# BTEC Introduction

# Travel & Tourism

# Hospitality

**www.heinemann.co.uk**

✓ Free online support
✓ Useful weblinks
✓ 24 hour online ordering

**01865 888058**

**Heinemann**

*Inspiring generations*

Heinemann Educational Publishers
Halley Court, Jordan Hill, Oxford OX2 8EJ
Part of Harcourt Education

Heinemann is a registered trademark of
Harcourt Education Limited

© Fiona Laing and Ian Roberts, 2005

First published 2005

10 09 08 07 06 05
10 9 8 7 6 5 4 3 2 1

British Library Cataloguing in Publication Data is available
from the British Library on request.

10-digit ISBN: 0 435 44631 2
13-digit ISBN: 978 0435446 31 4

Designed by Lorraine Inglis

Typeset and illustrated by Saxon Graphics Ltd

Original illustrations © Harcourt Education Limited, 2005

Printed by Scotprint Ltd
Cover photo: © Corbis
Picture research by Ruth Blair/Ginny Stroud–Lewis

**Websites**
Please note that the examples of websites suggested in this book were up to date at the time of
writing. It is essential for tutors to preview each site before using it to ensure that the URL is
still accurate and the content appropriate. To make this easier we have also made the links
available on the Heinemann website at www.heinemann.co.uk/hotlinks. When you access the
site, the express code is 6312P.

# Contents

# Acknowledgements

The authors and publishers are grateful to those who have given permission to reproduce material.

bmi, p13; Whitbread plc, p20; Caterer and Hotelkeeper, p37; Marriott Hotels, p44; McDonald's Restaurants of Ireland, p100; The Ritz, London, p168; Kosmar Holidays plc, p183; TUI UK Ltd, p183; Tradewinds Worldwide Holidays, p183; First Great Western Link, p184; Black Country Living Museum, p186; City Sightseeing Oxford/Tappins Coach Hire, p186; Beaulieu Enterprises Ltd, p186; Reed Business, p186 and p187; Thomas Cook, p191; VisitBritain, p219 and p220; Airtours Holidays, p222.

Crown copyright material is reproduced under Class Licence No. C02W0005419 with the permission of the Controller of HMSO and the Queen's Printer for Scotland.

## Photos

Photolibrary.com, p2(left); Corbis/Kelly-Mooney Photography, p2(right); AAF/Debbie Rowe, p7; Photolibrary.com, p8; Photolibrary.com, p10; AAF/Debbie Rowe, p12; Photodisc, p22; Alamy Images/David R. Frazier Photolibrary, Inc, p34; Alamy, p42; Alamy, 43; Rob Judges/Harcourt Education Ltd, p45; Getty Images/Photodisc, p68; Alamy Images/Dynamic Graphics Group/Creatas, p72; Getty Images/foodpix, p74; Getty Images/Taxi, p74; Corbis nrf, p96; Getty Images/Photodisc, p100; Harcourt Education Ltd/Gareth Boden, p111; Alamy, p119; Alamy Images/Bob Johns/expresspictures.co.uk, p124; Alamy Images/Peter Bowater, p125; Rob Judges/Harcourt Education Ltd, p132; Rob Judges/Harcourt Education Ltd, p136; Rob Judges/Harcourt Education Ltd, p137; Rob Judges/Harcourt Education Ltd, p139; Rob Judges/Harcourt Education Ltd; p141; Rob Judges/Harcourt Education Ltd, p143; Rob Judges/Harcourt Education Ltd, p144; Rob Judges/Harcourt Education Ltd, p147; Rob Judges/Harcourt Education Ltd, p150; Rob Judges/Harcourt Education Ltd, p151; Powerstock, p163; Alamy Images/The Hoberman Collection, p168; Corbis, p169; Alamy Images/Webstream, p172; AAF/Debbie Rowe, p194; Alamy, p197; Alamy Images/Travel Ink, p201; AAF/Debbie Rowe, p211; AAF/Debbie Rowe, p212; Art Directors and Trip, p213; AAF/Debbie Rowe, p215; AAF/Debbie Rowe, p219; Corbis nrf, p220; Corbis/Tom Stewart, p223.

Every effort has been made to contact copyright holders of material reproduced in this book. Any omissions will be rectified in subsequent printings if notice is given to the publishers.

# Introduction

This book has been written for students who are working towards the new BTEC Introductory Certificate or Diploma for Hospitality, Travel and Tourism. It covers the three core units, the three personal skills units and the four vocational option units for successful completion of these awards. The core units provide an introduction to the hospitality, travel and tourism industries and the skills required to work in these industries. The personal skills units will help you to prepare for work and the vocational optional units offer you more insight into the working world of hospitality, travel and tourism.

## The qualification

If you are working towards the Certificate you will need to successfully complete four units. If you are working towards the Diploma you will need to successfully complete eight units. Each unit consists of 30 or 60 hours of study. Unit 3 (core unit) and all the option units are 60-hour units.

For the **Certificate** you will need to cover:

**Core** – these are compulsory

 **Unit 1** Starting work in hospitality, travel and tourism

 **Unit 3** Introducing customer service

**Personal skills** – choose **one** of these units:

 **Unit 4** Personal effectiveness

 **Unit 5** Social responsibility at work

 **Unit 6** Financial management

**Vocational options** – choose **one** of these units:

 **Unit 7** The aspiring chef

 **Unit 8** Food service with a smile

 **Unit 9** Planning trips

 **Unit 10** Using displays in travel and tourism

For the **Diploma** you will need to cover:

**Core** – these are compulsory

 **Unit 1** Starting work in hospitality, travel and tourism

 **Unit 2** Working in hospitality, travel and tourism

 **Unit 3** Introducing customer service

**Personal skills** – choose **two** of these units:

**Unit 4**   Personal effectiveness

**Unit 5**   Social responsibility at work

**Unit 6**   Financial management

**Vocational options** – choose **three** of these units:

**Unit 7**   The aspiring chef

**Unit 8**   Food service with a smile

**Unit 9**   Planning trips

**Unit 10**  Using displays in travel and tourism

## • *Assessment and grading* •

All units except the personal skills units are graded as pass, merit or distinction.  Personal skills units are only graded as a pass.

For the certificate, Unit 1 is externally assessed.  For the diploma, Units 1 and 2 are externally assessed. This means you will complete a project set by Edexcel, the awarding body of this qualification. You can complete the project over a period of time, giving you plenty of chances to have your work checked and reviewed by your teaching staff. You can complete the project in a variety of ways, so choose a way which suits your working style the best. Your project will be internally assessed by your centre before being checked by an external BTEC verifier. The remaining units are internally assessed. This means, to pass the unit, you will complete an assignment set and marked by your tutor.

For each unit you must achieve a pass grade to achieve a qualification grade. The qualification is made up of units of 30 and 60 hours of learning. It is the grades awarded for the 60-hour units that will determine your grade for the qualification. For example, if you are taking the Certificate, your grade will be decided by your best performance of the two 60-hour units.  If you are taking the Diploma, your grade will be determined by your two best performances in the four 60-hour units.

The personal skills units and externally assessed units don't contribute towards your qualification grade.

## • *Putting together your portfolio* •

Your portfolio is an important document and needs to be put together with a clear structure to it. The evidence that it holds will determine whether you pass or fail, so keep it safe!

Your evidence may come in a variety of formats so your portfolio needs to be able to have in it the following:

- *Subject content, knowledge & understanding and associated skills*
- *Observer (witness) or personal statements*
- *Key skills and wider issues such as moral, spiritual & cultural issues*
- *Work experience*
- *Project reports*
- *Case studies*
- *Results of simulations or activities.*

If you gather evidence for one assignment which may also meet the needs of other learning outcomes you will need to carefully cross-reference the material. You should always remember that quality of material will always be valued above quantity. Your school or college may have a ready-made format, but you should take some tutor guidance on what is best. Make sure you look at the grade descriptors in the Unit so that you can match or target your efforts to achieve the best grade you can. Proper use of appropriate language will help, as will breadth and depth of knowledge in the right places. You may be asked some additional questions too, so be prepared.

Examiners will want to see that your evidence is:

- *Valid (appropriate)*
- *Reliable (consistent with real practice)*
- *Suitable (for the assessment needs).*

## Adult literacy, adult numeracy and key skills

The scheme also includes mapping of adult literacy, adult numeracy and Key Skills at level 1. The adult skills are for post-16 candidates only. The key skills are:

- *Application of number*
- *Communication*
- *Information technology*
- *Improving own learning and performance*
- *Problem solving*
- *Working with others*

## Special features in the book

There are a number of features throughout the text to encourage you to think about hospitality, travel and tourism. They also encourage you to find out information, undertake activities and gather evidence towards your assessment.

*Case studies*: These are real-life (or simulated) situations involving customers and people working in hospitality, travel and tourism. The questions that follow each case study give you the opportunity to look at important issues and widen your understanding of the subject.

 *Give it a go*: Issues relevant to hospitality, travel and tourism are raised for you to discuss or work through either with a partner, in groups or on your own.

 *What if? …* These present situations which may arise and provide you with opportunities for problem solving.

 *Think about it*: These are thought-provoking questions about issues or dilemmas that are relevant in hospitality, travel and tourism. They can be done individually or in groups.

 *Evidence activity*: These are activities that provide you with practise evidence to show that you understand the work required in the unit.  By working through the activities you will gain evidence to meet the grading criteria for each unit at pass, merit or distinction grade - or only a pass grade for personal skills units.

Other features included in this book are:

- **Key terms** are picked out and explained where they occur in the text. This helps to make clear any jargon (specialised language) used.
- an end-of-unit **knowledge check** and wordsearch. This allows you to recap on the knowledge you have learnt throughout the unit. You are then asked to find the answers to the questions which are hidden in a wordsearch.

This book has been written by people with experience of the hospitality, travel and tourism industries who have a commitment to encouraging you to consider a career in one of these areas. We wish you the best of luck on your course as you begin your journey towards a career in hospitality or travel and tourism. We hope you find this book stimulating and useful.

Fiona Laing and Ian Roberts

# unit 1

## Starting work in hospitality, travel and tourism

Hospitality, travel and tourism are three exciting industries that have many similarities and connections to each other. These industries employ a workforce of around 4 million people. The area offers a huge range of exciting and rewarding job opportunities. This unit has been designed to help you find out what it is like to work in this area and the jobs that are available in different organisations. Many people work in all three industries during their career, while others choose to specialise within one specific area – such as a career working as a tour guide in the Greek Islands.

*In this unit you will learn about:*

⬭ the different types of jobs in hospitality, travel and tourism
⬭ how the different types of organisations in this area might affect your choice of job
⬭ the relationship between your lifestyle and job choices.

# Different types of jobs

Within the hospitality, travel and tourism sector there is an enormous range of job roles and employment opportunities. This section will look at some of these roles in detail.

## GIVE IT A GO: jobs in hospitality, travel and tourism

1 Working with a partner, can you list three jobs for each industry?

2 Do any of these jobs appeal to you? Do you like the idea of being a tour guide? Or a waiter in a fancy restaurant? Or a chef in a busy kitchen? With your partner, discuss what you think you would like about doing these jobs.

## Job roles in hospitality

What do people in hospitality do? The picture below shows a range of roles that you will find in a busy hospitality organisation. In this section you will investigate what these different roles involve.

## GIVE IT A GO: name the job roles

Can you identify the different job roles shown in the pictures above?

## ● *Chef* ●

A chef is a professional cook – someone who cooks food for his or her living. A chef usually works in a team preparing and cooking food for people who are paying for their meals. There is a lot more to it than just cooking food for people though! A chef needs to have imagination, good practical skills and stamina. Imagine having to cook the same dish for 400 people – a professional chef might well have to!

As a chef you could work in a variety of places. You might work in a restaurant, a large or small hotel, a theme park or another visitor attraction. Alternatively a chef's job might be **service based**, such as in a hospital, a prison, a school or college or a canteen in a large office. The list is endless as to the types and varieties of place that offer food to the public – and all of these places need chefs to help with this task.

> **GLOSSARY**
>
> **Service based** means providing a service to people in an organisation.

### GIVE IT A GO: famous foods

A chef might cook many dishes from around the world. Do you know what the following dishes are? With a partner, check that you understand what each dish is and where the dish comes from:

| | | | | |
|---|---|---|---|---|
| Coq au vin | Pavlova | Fondu | Steak and kidney pie | Chilli |
| Goulash | Paella | Moussaka | Risotto | Tandoori |
| Enchiladas | Profiteroles | Sushi | Korma | |

The type of cooking a chef will do depends on the style of restaurant or hotel, what sort of menu is offered to guests and the price they pay. Sometimes, there is only minimum preparation, because some foods are commonly brought in by a supplier, such as stocks, some desserts and certain breads and pastries. No less skill is required to produce a perfectly cooked, well-presented dish. High standards of hygiene, good knife skills and accuracy in measuring ingredients and portion sizes are all essential. Duties may also include dealing with deliveries, stock rotation and requisitioning of stock.

Job titles and responsibilities vary in different organisations. Where might you start? **Commis chef** is the starting position for a career in hotel and restaurant kitchens. In this role you do a lot of the preparation work and basic cooking, working under the **supervision** of more experienced chefs. Ideally, while you are training, you move around to work in the different areas of the kitchen. This allows you to get the widest possible experience before you think about what area you might like to specialise in, such as **pastry work**.

> **GLOSSARY**
>
> A **commis chef** is a trainee or junior chef. **Supervision** means being watched over while you are doing a task at your workplace. **Pastry work** is any work for sweets and desserts, and also the pastry work for making tops to savoury pies, such as steak and kidney.

## GIVE IT A GO: the chef's role

1 Working with a partner, make a list of questions you would like to ask a professional chef about the work he or she does each day.

2 Do you know anyone who works as a chef? If you do, try to find a chance to talk to them and ask them your questions.

▲ Chefs earn a living by cooking food for other people

There is a very important, serious role to think about as a chef – hygiene. By law, chefs are responsible for making sure that the food they prepare and cook for people is safe to eat. If a chef gets this wrong, he or she could end up causing the death of a customer. One of the laws that covers food handling and production is called The Food Safety Act 1990. You will learn more about this in Unit 7.

## GIVE IT A GO: restaurants in your area

1 Working with a partner, research the range of restaurants in your local area. You may also find information in the Yellow Pages, your local press or on the Internet. Produce a list in an appropriate IT format that clearly shows the different types of restaurants, e.g. Mexican, French and English.

2 If possible, visit some of these restaurants to collect a record of the food they offer on their menus. Add this research to your IT file.

3 With your tutor's help prepare a short presentation that explains the range of restaurants in your area and some of the most popular dishes that are offered by them. Make sure that you are able to explain all the dishes on offer.

## ● *Food service staff* ●

When the chefs have prepared and cooked the food, all the dishes have to be delivered to the customer in the best possible condition. This needs to be done in an efficient, safe and hygienic manner. The type of food service will depend on the type of outlet. For example, at a top-class restaurant you can expect full **silver service**, but a canteen might be self-service.

Food service is a skilled professional role. The waiting staff need to understand:

- *what is available to serve or sell to the customer*
- *what accompaniments should be offered with the food/beverages*
- *how to take a customer's order*
- *how to prepare, maintain and clear away the food service area*
- *how to keep the food service area safe and hygienic.*

Whatever the method of service used by the **catering establishment**, any waiting staff are going to need to have the following qualities if they are to be successful:

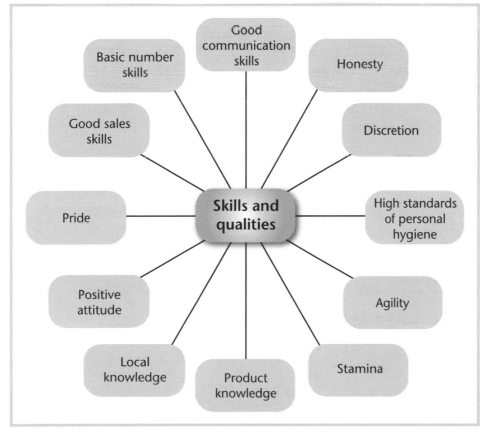

▲ **Skills and qualities needed in food service staff**

### GLOSSARY

**Food service** means serving foods and beverages to customers.
**Silver service** is a style of food service where all food is served to the customer by a member of waiting staff from a serving dish using a spoon and fork.

### GLOSSARY

A **catering establishment** is a business that provides food and drink to the public.

### GLOSSARY

**Discretion** means knowing when not to repeat something you have overheard or when not to say anything at all in a social situation.
**Agility** is the ability to move quickly and easily.
**Sales** skills are techniques you use to convince a customer to buy something.

## GIVE IT A GO: a good waiter

Consider the skills and qualities in the diagram on page 5. Why do you think that they would be important for waiting staff? Using a word processor, write a short description of the skills you think food service staff would need to do their job and the reasons why.

▲ Waiting staff may often overhear things that they should not!

## ● *Bar person* ●

### GLOSSARY

**Non-alcoholic beverages** are drinks that do not contain alcohol, such as coffee, tea, cola and squash.

Staff who work in the bar area selling alcoholic and **non-alcoholic beverages** require special skills. Customers will visit a bar wherever it is located, if they like the products being sold, the atmosphere and the service. Staff must be able to show a welcoming attitude towards all customers at all times – not always an easy thing to do! Bar staff must be sociable with very good communication skills.

In the UK, in order to be employed in any area that sells alcoholic drinks, you need to be over 18 years of age. Bar staff also need a good level of knowledge of alcoholic and non-alcoholic drinks. Bar staff may work in a variety of establishments including pubs, nightclubs, licensed clubs, cruise ships, hotels, restaurants and many more.

## WHAT

### ... *you had to deal with a customer who was drunk?*

Imagine you are working in a busy bar and you are faced with a female customer who begins shouting at you that she has been waiting a long time to be served. She appears to have had quite a bit to drink and begins to shake her fist and swear at you.

- How would you handle this situation?
- In a suitable IT format, produce a handout to give new staff guidance on what to do in such a situation.

## ● *Receptionist* ●

A reception is usually the first point of contact for anyone entering an organisation. It is here that the vital first impressions are created.

▲ **The receptionist creates vital first impressions**

Receptionists greet visitors to the organisation and deal with their queries. Their role will differ depending on the type of organisation. Reception may also be referred to as Front Office. In a hotel, a receptionist may be responsible for taking room bookings, dealing with guests' queries, taking payment and exchanging foreign currency. In a large travel organisation, receptionists may work the switchboard and direct incoming calls.

A reception is like the centre of a wheel. It is linked to every area of the organisation. Information to and from all of the other departments passes through reception.

▲ **Reception is linked to every area of the organisation**

## • *Room service attendant/housekeeper* •

Room service attendants are in charge of the cleanliness of all the guest rooms and most of, if not all, the public areas. Working as part of a team under the head housekeeper, they use special equipment, such as industrial vacuum cleaners, shampooers, polishers and trolleys. Room attendants need to keep the equipment they use in good condition and learn how to use it safely.

▲ Room service adds to the feeling of luxury

Room attendants will often be given their own floor or area to clean. Completing the work efficiently, (quickly and well), is an important skill. They must make sure the rooms are in a first-class condition for both new guests as they arrive and guests on continued stays – this is vital for customer satisfaction. They need to liaise with the head housekeeper to keep him or her informed as rooms become ready to let to new guests.

## EVIDENCE ACTIVITY P1

### Job roles in hospitality

1 Using the Internet, investigate the opportunities for employment that there might be within the hospitality industry. You may find the websites of the following organisations useful:

British Hospitality Association  Hotel and Catering International Management Association
Caterer and Hotelkeeper  Hospitality Net
The Catering Net  Hospitality Training Foundation
  Whitbread

Links to these sites are available through www.heinemann.co.uk/hotlinks (express code 6312P, then go to Unit 1).

2 Using IT, produce a list describing the range of roles you find.

## Job roles in travel and tourism

Did you know tourism is set to become the world's largest industry by 2010? You will now investigate a variety of job roles in this dynamic and growing industry.

## GIVE IT A GO: name the job roles

Look at the picture above of a busy travel and tourism scene. Can you identify and name the different job roles?

## • *Tour guide* •

A tour guide is a specialist guide responsible for taking a group of visitors and holidaymakers around a specific area, including interesting sites in that area. Tour guides are usually employed by **tour operators**, such as Club Med. They represent the tour operator and ensure that customers get the best from their holiday experience. A tour guide could also be a local guide working **freelance**.

A tour guide's job involves organising, promoting and leading tours through areas of interest. The tour guide informs the guests about particular points of interest and answers questions. He or she is also responsible for making sure that adequate transportation is ready and that all the guests are prepared for the particular excursion.

### UK tour guides

In the UK, tour guides are sometimes Blue Badge registered guides. This means that The Guild of Registered Tourist Guides has selected, trained and examined the guide. Blue Badge registration means that a guide is experienced, has specialist knowledge and may be able to speak other languages. You can find out more about Blue Badge registration by visiting The Guild of Registered Tourist Guides website (go to www.heine-mann.co.uk/hotlinks, enter express code 6312P and then go to Unit 1).

### GLOSSARY

**Tour operators** are the organisations that produce holiday packages to sell to customers.
**A freelance** is someone who works for lots of different companies.

Walking tours around cities are very popular. Many of these often have a specific theme, such as the Oxford Ghost Tour!

### The Oxford Ghost Tour

Discover the dark side of Oxford's past in a spine-chilling guided walking tour of the city's streets, colleges and pubs.
Tremble to the tales of:
• Oxford's own vampire
• The headless king
• The haunted pubs and colleges
• Witchcraft and sorcery and much, much more

Tour starts from the Oxfam shop on Broad Street, every night at 9.00pm.

▲ Some tour guides work in the evening

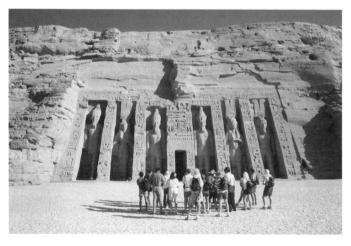

▲ Tour guides often need specialist knowledge

### Overseas tour guides

Many different types of travel organisation offer tour services. Coach tours are probably the most common. Other popular short tours include:

- *river and lake cruises*
- *light aircraft or helicopter rides over spectacular scenery*
- *city tours in open-top buses or horse-drawn carriages*
- *walking tours*
- *steam train rides.*

## GIVE IT A GO: fancy working abroad?

Write a short list of the advantages and disadvantages that you think there might be of working abroad as a tour guide.

## • *Retail travel agent* •

A retail travel agent is someone who works in a company selling holidays directly to the public. A travel agent might work for a small part of a larger organisation. For example, they might work for the travel agent Going Places, which is part of the larger company Airtours.

### GIVE IT A GO: travel agencies in your high street

1 Working with a partner, can you think of the names of any high street travel agencies? You may even have booked holidays using some of them.
2 List the services that are usually offered by a high street travel agency.

To work as a travel agent you need to have specific skills. You need good sales and customer service skills and basic IT skills. Knowledge of the travel and tourism industry and **market** is an advantage.

Some tasks carried out by travel agency staff would include:

- *advising customers on holiday choices available*
- *checking prices and availability of holidays with tour operators*
- *supplying foreign currency, traveller's cheques and holiday insurance*
- *issuing tickets*
- *keeping reservation records up to date.*

> **GLOSSARY**
>
> The **market** is the area or people you are selling or offering your products to.

### GIVE IT A GO: the travel agent's role

Working with a partner, produce a short presentation to give to your group (maybe using Microsoft® PowerPoint) that details the types of tasks carried out on a day-to-day basis by a retail travel agent.

## • *Visitor attraction guide* •

When people are thinking about taking a holiday, short break or day trip, there are all kinds of places that they can choose from. In travel and tourism the place a tourist visits is called the destination. As you might imagine, travel and tourism is a very **competitive business**. There needs to be a reason to make people decide to travel to a particular destination. One reason is the **visitor attractions**. Different destinations are famous for their particular visitor attractions. For example, most people visit Orlando, in the USA, because they want to spend some time at Disneyworld.

> **GLOSSARY**
>
> **A competitive business** is one where there are lots of similar products available for customers to choose from.
> **A visitor attraction** is a place, building or leisure facility that is popular with tourists.

## CASE STUDY – WORKING AS A RETAIL TRAVEL AGENT

To sort out the many travel options, tourists and business people often turn to travel agents to help them make the best possible travel arrangements. Also, many major cruise lines, resorts, and specialty travel groups use travel agents to promote travel packages to millions of people every year.

In general, travel agents give advice on destinations and make arrangements for transportation, hotel accommodation, car rentals and tours. They may also advise on weather conditions, restaurants, tourist attractions, and recreation. For international travel, agents also provide information on customs **regulations**, required papers (passports, visas, and certificates of vaccination), and currency exchange rates.

Travel agents consult a variety of published and computer-based sources for information on departure and arrival times, fares, hotel ratings and accommodations. They may visit hotels, resorts, and restaurants to evaluate quality. Depending on the size of the travel agency, an agent may specialise by type of travel, such as leisure or business, or destination, such as Europe or Africa.

● Why do people choose to use travel agents to help them arrange their holidays?

### GLOSSARY

**Regulations** are rules that a person or company must follow.

Museums, art galleries, theme parks, wildlife attractions and heritage centres all employ guides to help visitors get the most out of their experience. Visitor guides can offer people expert knowledge about the attraction. For example, STEAM, the museum of the Great Western Railway in Swindon, has specialist visitor guides who are on hand to explain the museum and its trains to visitors. All of the guides are ex-workers who spent many years working in the railway factory that was once on the site of the museum.

Visitor guides can also help with other practical information about the facilities, such as where the nearest toilet is, and local information, such as the nearest cash point.

◀ **The London Eye – a popular UK visitor attraction**

## GIVE IT A GO: Paris

When people travel to Paris, in France, one of the attractions that they may want to visit is the Eiffel Tower.

**1** Can you list two other attractions in Paris that people visit?

**2** What kind of attractions are these?

## GIVE IT A GO: skills for the job

Using some of the knowledge you have gained so far in this unit, make a list of the skills and qualities a visitor attraction guide needs for his or her role.

## ● *Airport customer service agent* ●

The role of customer service agent is vital for many organisations but particularly in the often highly stressful and emotional world of airport reservation, check-ins, arrivals and departures. People use airports for a variety of reasons. For example, they might be going on a holiday that they have looked forward to all year and has cost them a lot of money. They might be travelling because of a family illness or bereavement. They could be on a very important business trip.

Under these stressed conditions people can often be demanding, impatient and sometimes downright rude. In this kind of atmosphere it takes skilful staff with a lot of training to keep calm and still be able to help the customers.

## CASE STUDY – bmi CUSTOMER SERVICE AGENT

One of the UK's leading scheduled airlines, we operate 1,700 flights a week to 37 destinations in 14 countries and an international network reaching all areas of the globe.

As a Customer Service Agent you'll be an ambassador for the airline, part of a friendly team with a flexible attitude to work. Performing a varied workload you'll need stamina and dedication to deliver exceptional customer service on a tight schedule and a character that can smile through any situation. We can offer you ample training and we'll encourage you to develop your career.

So what are we looking for? You'll be a minimum age of 18 and hold a full clean drivers licence. On top of a good standard of education (four GCSEs at grade C or above including Maths and English or equivalent),

you'll bring excellent people skills, personal confidence and the flexibility to work shifts. Ideally you will have a minimum of 12 months' experience in a customer-facing role. You will also be required to undertake a satisfactory criminal record check and obtain a certificate that is acceptable to the company and regulatory authorities.

Source: www.aviationjobsearch.com

1 Give an example of another job in hospitality, travel and tourism that would provide suitable experience in a customer-facing role.

2 Explain what being 'an ambassador for the airline' means.

3 Explain one situation where a customer service agent would need 'a character that can smile through any situation'.

## • *Tourist information guide* •

The role of tourist information guide involves providing information to the public about the tourist destination they work in. They are often employed in areas abroad that receive large numbers of British tourists, such as France and Spain. The larger cities and tourist attractions in the UK, such as London or the Cheddar Gorge, would also use tourist information guides to ensure that visitors received the most reliable and accurate information about the place they are visiting.

Tourist information guides would be expected to know about the range of attractions in their area. They would not need to have detailed knowledge of each visitor attraction. They need to be very knowledgeable about local information, such as transport and where banks can be found.

## GIVE IT A GO: tourists' inquiries

Write a list of five questions that a customer might ask on visiting a tourist information centre.

## WHAT if?

### ... you worked in a tourist information centre?

As a tourist information guide you need to know your subject.
If you worked in the UK, you would need to have knowledge of the whole country. Can you locate the following regions on the map of the UK?

- West Country
- Cotswolds
- Wales
- Highlands
- East Anglia
- London
- Scotland
- Lake District
- Yorkshire
- Peak District.

## EVIDENCE ACTIVITY    P1

### Jobs in travel and tourism

1  Using the Internet, investigate the employment opportunities that there might be within travel and tourism.

2  Using IT, write a list describing the range of roles you find.

# Types of job

As well as a huge choice of jobs within hospitality, travel and tourism, there are also a large variety of types of employment. You might choose to work full time but that is certainly not the only option. You will find different types of job in different organisations:

| Types of Job | What this means |
|---|---|
| Part time | You work a limited number of hours a week. For example, you might work 15 hours a week, from 11am–2pm Monday to Friday. |
| Full time | You work a specified number of hours each week, usually 35 or 37 hours a week. |
| Temporary | You work for an employer for a short period only, such as three months. You may be either part time or full time. |
| Permanent | You work for an employer long term and do not have a fixed date when the job will end. |
| Seasonal | You work during a specific season, such as winter. |
| Live-in | Your job provides you with accommodation. |
| Freelance | You work for yourself and organisations hire you to work on specific jobs. |
| Skilled/Operative | You need specific skills to carry out your job. |
| Unskilled | You do not need any specific skills to do your work. |
| Craft | Your job involves making things by hand. |
| Supervisory | You oversee the work of other staff. |

**GIVE IT A GO: types of job**

Can you identify at least one job role as an example for each of the categories listed in the table?

# Personal requirements

What sort of person do you need to be to work in hospitality, leisure and tourism? Some of the important personal qualities and skills are shown in the diagram on page 16.

## THINK ABOUT IT

Can you work as part of a team? Do you work well with others? Do you listen to others? Can you be patient working with others? Are you reliable? If you answer 'yes' to all of these questions, you may be good at working as part of a team.

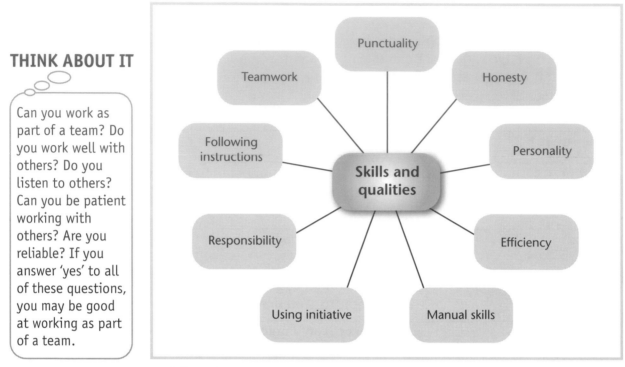

▲ Skills and qualities needed in hospitality, travel and tourism

## GIVE IT A GO: skills and why they are important

Look at the diagram of personal qualities and skills above. Why do you think that they would be important to any person working in hospitality, travel and tourism? Discuss your ideas with a partner and check with your tutor that you have understood each one.

Firstly, and most importantly, you need to like people and enjoy the challenge of working with others. You need to be flexible, adaptable and enjoy problem solving and thinking on your feet. You also need to be able to work as part of a team.

## GIVE IT A GO: matching skills and qualities to a job

Read the following job description.

As a trainee chef you will help to prepare food such as vegetables, salads, meat and fish depending on the area you are working in. You will be involved in some basic cooking and possibly help with more advanced dishes under the supervision of a senior chef. Your duties will also include helping clean and maintain hygiene within the kitchen.

With a partner, make a list of the skills and qualities you would need to do this job.

## EVIDENCE ACTIVITY

### *Skills and jobs*

1 Building on your work earlier in the unit, consider the following skills and qualities. Link them to jobs in hospitality, travel and tourism where they might be used. Copy and complete the table. **P2**

| Skill/quality | Reason it is important | Example of job where the skill/quality might be used |
|---|---|---|
| Punctuality | | |
| Personality | | |
| Initiative | | |
| Communication skills | | |
| Honesty | | |
| Manual skills | | |
| Efficiency | | |
| Responsibility | | |
| Teamwork | | |
| Ability to follow instructions | | |
| Positive attitude | | |
| Ability to sell | | |

2 Prepare a report that describes the range of jobs you identified in the GIVE IT A GO activity on page 2, together with the skills and qualities needed across the hospitality, travel and tourism. **M1**

3 Identify the type of job you would like to do. Explain which specific skills and qualities would be needed to successfully undertake this job role and why they are needed. **D1**

# Different types of organisation

The hospitality, travel and tourism sector is made up of an enormous range of organisations. This is hardly surprising when you think that it is one of the world's biggest employment sectors.

In this section you will look at the different types of organisations and how they are structured, and think about their different locations.

# EVICENCE ACTIVITY  P3

## Types of organisation

1 Looking back over your work in this unit, with a partner create a table similar to the one below to show all the organisations that can provide employment. Give specific examples of organisations within your local area or others that you are familiar with.

| Hospitality | Travel and Tourism |
|---|---|
| **1** restaurants<br><br>e.g. ................................. | **1** visitor attractions<br><br>e.g. ................................. |
| 2 | 2 |
| 3 | 3 |
| 4 | 4 |
| 5 | 5 |

2 When you have completed the table ask your tutor to make sure that you have a good range of organisations within this huge industry.

# The structure of organisations

Organisations come in many shapes and sizes. They can be very small and simple with only one person in the company or they may take the form of a huge multinational company employing thousands of people in different countries.

## • Private •

Private organisations are those owned by one person, one family or one group of people. Most organisations in hospitality, travel and tourism fall into this category. Private organisations aim to make money. Longleat stately home and safari park in Wiltshire is an example of a privately owned organisation, home to the 7th Marquess of Bath. Airtours plc is another example of a private company, which is owned by a number of people who **invest** in the company. You can find out more about Longleat and Airtours by visiting their websites (go to www.heinemann.co.uk/hotlinks, enter express code 6312P then go to Unit 1).

### GLOSSARY

When someone **invests** in a company they put money into the company and get a share of any profits.

18

## • *Public* •

Public organisations are those that are **funded** and operated by the government. The Department of Media, Culture and Sport and the Countryside Commision are examples of public organisations that have connections with the hospitality, travel and tourism industries.

**GLOSSARY**

**To fund** means to give an organisation money.

## • *Non profit-making* •

An organisation that is there to provide a service rather than make a profit is a non-profit-making organisation. Many of the cultural heritage organisations, such as Tourism Concern and The Ramblers Association, as well as the Youth Hostels Association are in this category.

## • *Sole proprietor* •

This is the simplest form of setting up and running a business and is also referred to as 'a sole trader'. This structure of organisation is most suited to small businesses, such as bed and breakfasts. The sole trader owns the business, takes all the risks, suffers any losses and keeps any profits.

## • *Partnership* •

A partnership consists of two or more people working together as the owners of a business. A partnership is similar to a sole trader in that the partners own the business and take all the risks. If the business fails, the partners will lose the money they have invested.

## • *Franchise* •

A franchise allows people to set up an outlet of a well-established company. Over 70 per cent of McDonald's restaurants are franchises. People invest their own money in the company. They then run the business and keep some of the profits. They also benefit from the support that a large multinational company like McDonald's can provide.

## • *Limited company* •

In these companies the financial risk of the owners is limited. This means that should the business run into financial trouble and have to close, the amount of debt it would owe to people who had invested in it would be *limited*. This is done to encourage business people to take the risks in the first place to set up companies and businesses. If they knew they would have to pay everything back to everyone should they get into trouble, less people would take such a risk and fewer businesses would be started. There are two types:

▷ *Private limited company – used for smaller and medium-sized organisations. These companies are privately owned.*

▭ *Public limited company – used for larger businesses. The shares can be bought by the general public. The words public limited company must appear in the company's name. (This may be abbreviated to PLC.) These organisations are usually big businesses made up of many **brands**.*

## • *Multinational* •

A multinational organisation operates in more than one country. You have already looked at the example of McDonald's. Other examples include Virgin and Intercontinental Hotels.

## CASE STUDY – WHITBREAD PLC

**Whitbread**
*Welcome with a smile*

Whitbread PLC is the UK's leading leisure business, managing some of the UK's strongest brands in hotels, restaurants and health and fitness clubs. Our employees deliver outstanding service to millions of customers each month at more than 1900 locations across the UK.

Whitbread brands include Travel Inn, Marriott, Brewers Fayre, Brewsters, Beefeater, Out & Out, Pizza Hut, Costa, TGI Friday's and David Lloyd Leisure.

With such a wide selection of restaurants, hotels and sports, health and fitness clubs, there's plenty of opportunity at Whitbread for those wanting to build a career within the leisure industry.

Whitbread now has around 40,000 employees working in its restaurants, hotels, health clubs and service departments. In order to attract and retain the best staff, Whitbread's **commitment** to caring for and developing its people is one of the company's most important concerns.

In 2004, Whitbread's businesses achieved success in the Sunday Times 'Great Place to Work' and Financial Times 'Best Workplace in the UK' surveys. Whitbread Restaurants was the winner of the Young People Award category, for it's Chef Recruitment Programme and TGI Friday's was the winner for Best Careers Progression and **Retention**.

The Work Foundation – formerly the Industrial Society – recently applauded Whitbread as an employer that can claim with good evidence to be a company with an emphasis on treating staff well.

Source: www.whitbread.co.uk

1  List six different employment roles that are available within Whitbread.

2  Why is Whitbread so keen to attract and keep new staff?

3  Why is Whitbread so keen to promote the employment awards it has recently won?

GLOSSARY

**Commitment** refers to the effort a company is prepared to put in to its staff, such as providing them with good training or working conditions.

**Retention** means keeping employees over a long period of time.

## GIVE IT A GO: types of organisation

1 Working on your own research and produce a list of ten organisations in your area that are part of the hospitality, travel and tourism sector.

2 What kind of organisations are they (e.g. franchise, multinational)?

3 State the reasons why you would or would not wish to work for them.

## EVIDENCE ACTIVITY

### *Organisations in the hospitality, travel and tourism sector*

1 Research a local business that operates in the hospitality industry, where you could find a job that appeals to you. Using IT, write a brief summary that includes: **P4**

   • what kind of organisation or establishment it is

   • a brief history of the company

   • what it does

   • the areas of business in which it operates

   • the types of job opportunities that the company can provide.

2 Produce a table that shows the type of organisations operating across hospitality, travel and tourism. Indicate which organisation works in which area and those that are involved across both. Show whether the organisation is local, national or international. **M2**

# Location of organisations and employment

From a small bed and breakfast in the heart of the countryside to a city centre hotel, organisations that provide hospitality, travel and tourism are based anywhere there is a need. Locations include:

▷ *city – based in a city, e.g. a hotel in a large capital city*
▷ *urban – based in major towns and cities, e.g. Wetherspoons and Pizza Hut*
▷ *rural – based in countryside locations, e.g. a country health spa*
▷ *seaside – based on the coast, e.g. specialist seafood restaurants with a menu full of fresh fish and shellfish*
▷ *regional variations – based in a particular area of the country, e.g. the Magpie café fish and chips restaurant in Whitby or Strada's, a chain of Italian restaurants, located in London and the South*
▷ *European – based across Europe*
▷ *international – based worldwide, the most obvious example being McDonald's.*

▲ **You may need your own transport to work here**

As a professional working in hospitality, travel and tourism, you might choose to work in any of these locations during your career.

## Accessibility and proximity to home

Another factor to consider is where the workplace is and how easy is it to get to. As we have discussed, hospitality, travel and tourism organisations are found throughout the world in every conceivable location. Some are extremely easy to get to, such as those in city centres that are well supported by transport links like roads, bus routes and train services. Others can be in the middle of nowhere and very difficult to get to and from. A country pub that can only be reached by road will not be a viable employer for someone with no car and who does not live close enough to walk or cycle to and from work.

# Lifestyle and jobs in hospitality, travel and tourism

### Effect of lifestyle on job

Your current lifestyle will influence your choice of job. While most people need to work to earn a living, they will still be able to decide how they earn this money. Their choices will suit their preferred lifestyle and their individual wants and needs.

As you saw in the last section, the location of the workplace will play a part. Personal circumstances might mean you cannot be flexible in your choice of location to work in. For example, if you do not drive, it would be difficult for you to take a job in a small country pub that is not on a public transport route.

You might have commitments and personal relationships, like Janita in the case study below, that limit the hours you are available to work. You may not want to work the hours and shifts that are involved in some jobs in hospitality, travel and tourism or you might find that these hours suit you perfectly.

Your ambitions, where you want to go in life, and your career dreams will also be an important factor. You might love the social side of a career in hospitality, travel and tourism because of what it adds to your lifestyle.

## CASE STUDY – BREAKFAST CHEF

Janita is employed as a breakfast chef at a small hotel and restaurant on the outskirts of Birmingham. The hotel is particularly busy Monday to Friday, with a healthy trade in businessmen and women who stay in the hotel while visiting Birmingham. Janita is employed to start work at 6 am for breakfast service and then works through until 2.30 pm, when she helps during the lunchtime period of service. With breaks, Janita still works enough hours to make up a full-time job, but finishes work each day during the week by 3 pm.

- Why does the hotel provide breakfast and lunchtime services, rather than focusing on evening meals as some other establishments might do?
- Janita has two children aged 7 and 8. How might this job suit her and her lifestyle? What problems might she have?

## EVIDENCE ACTIVITY     P5

### Choosing a job

Make a short list of the factors in any young person's lifestyle (it could be your own) that might affect the choice of job within the hospitality, travel and tourism sector.

## Effect of job on lifestyle

Your job will always have an impact on your lifestyle and this is certainly the case in hospitality, travel and tourism.

There are many job-related issues that can have an effect on your lifestyle including:

- *the number of hours you work*
- *the times these hours of work take place*
- *where you work*
- *how much you are paid for the work*
- *the pressures that may be involved in the work*
- *whether the job is a desk job or involves any physically demanding work.*

## GIVE IT A GO: air cabin crew

Imagine you were employed as a member of an airline's cabin crew. List the advantages and disadvantages that you think your job might bring to your lifestyle.

### • *Hours of work* •

The hospitality, travel and tourism sector does not always offer the more traditional 9–5 approach to employment! Many people have preferred lifestyles that may mean that some roles in hospitality, travel and tourism would not be suitable for them. If someone cannot or does not want to work at weekends or can only work set hours during the day, being a tour guide would be out of the question, for example.

## GIVE IT A GO: who's not cut out for it?

List any other reasons relating to a person's lifestyle that might stop them from working in certain job roles in hospitality, travel and tourism.

### • *Stress levels* •

Many jobs in the hospitality, travel and tourism sector involve working under pressure. For example, if you have ever seen the BBC programme *Airport*, you will be aware of the stressful situations customer service staff sometimes find themselves in. Being in a position where you could be shouted at by a group of angry customers whose flight has been delayed is not for the faint-hearted!

### • *Physical and other limitations* •

Some work is quite demanding physically, such as some aspects of kitchen work or baggage handling. Pilots are required to have good eyesight. You should consider whether the physical challenges of a job are something that you could or would want to cope with when deciding on a career. The sector is so varied in the types of jobs available that there is usually a role to suit any person.

## ● *Personal and professional ambitions* ●

There are other things that might affect how you think about your job.
These include:

- *how much you need to earn*
- *what your long-term ambitions are*
- *whether your personal skills and qualities are being used*
- *what training or professional qualifications and studying you will need to undertake.*

### Need to earn a living

All people are different and so are their lifestyles and personal needs.
How much you need to earn can affect the type of job you are willing to
do. For example, if you have a partner who is also working you might
not need to earn as much as a single person. If you have family responsibilities you might look for a job with good pay and career prospects.

### Personal ambitions

It is also very important to consider your personal ambitions when
looking for employment. What do you want in terms of a job or a
career? All people are different with different needs and ambitions in
life. For example, rather than being focused on the amount of money
you will earn, you might have a burning desire to travel the world and
see working in travel and tourism as a way to achieve this ambition.

### Training

If you want to gain professional qualifications and progress into
management you might find a career in hotels is the way to do this.

### Personal skills

Anyone considering a career in hospitality, travel and tourism needs to
think about their own personal skills and qualities. For example, if you
are very shy and dislike face-to-face conversations with others, you may
not be the most suitable person to apply for the post of customer service
agent. Equally, if you know that your organisational skills are not the
best you might not be cut out for work in a busy hotel reception.

## CASE STUDY – TOUR GUIDE

Anna works as a tour guide in India and is employed by the **direct-sell** tour operator Travelsphere. A typical example of the type of tours Anna leads is the 18-day tour of India, which takes in such major cities as Agra, Delhi, Jaipur and Bangalore. Attractions the tour visits include such places as the Taj Mahal, Delhi's Red Fort and the Temple of Kali in Jaipur.

Anna has a detailed knowledge of not only the places and attractions, but also the local customs and the accepted forms of behaviour and dress for visitors, which she passes on to the tourists travelling with her. Working directly with customers, Anna's personal skills are as important as her knowledge.

Anna starts work very early in the morning. Long before the tourists get up she is preparing for the day's work. She has no time 'off duty' during the tour. These demands mean that the job has some very definite impacts on Anna's lifestyle, but equally it offers her the chance for many rewards and lots of job satisfaction.

**1** Why are Anna's personal skills as important as her knowledge of the destinations and attractions when accompanying tourists?

**2** Why is Anna unlikely to be off duty throughout the tour?

**4** What effects has Anna's job choice had on her lifestyle do you think?

### GLOSSARY

**Direct-sell** means they sell to customers directly rather than using travel agents.

## GIVE IT A GO: looking for a job?

Read the two job adverts below.

The Langston Arms Hotel is looking to appoint a full time receptionist to assist the Front Office team at this prestigious, city centre hotel. We seek a professional, friendly and hard-working team player who can communicate well with both staff and customers. IT skills would be helpful but not essential as full training will be provided.

CinnamonTravel are looking for outgoing, hardworking individuals with a developed sense of responsibility to work as tour guides at one of our busy holiday resorts in Majorca. Full training will be provided. Please visit our website for an online application form.

**1** Would you like to apply for either of these jobs?

**2** What skills and qualities would you need to have to do these jobs?

**3** What type of training do you think you would be given if you got either job?

**4** How do you think the qualification in hospitality, travel and tourism you are completing will help you in these jobs?

## CASE STUDY – A DAY IN THE LIFE OF A RESORT REPRESENTATIVE

Andy is a resort representative for a large travel company. A typical day looks something like this:

| | |
|---|---|
| 8.45–9am | See group of tourists onto a coach for an excursion. |
| 9–10am | Andy's first visit to a local hotel where the travel company has customers staying. Andy meets the guests for a welcome session to discuss any issues or answer any queries. |
| 10–11am | Visit another hotel where the company has guests. Some guests have questions and problems which Andy helps to resolve. |
| 11am–1pm | Administration and paperwork. |
| 1–3pm | Andy helps with a hotel pick-up, which involves taking a coach to the hotels where |

customers are staying and then taking the customers to the airport for their flight home.

| | |
|---|---|
| 3–4.30pm | Arrive at airport. Andy helps customers with their check in and makes sure they get to their departure gate. |
| 4.30–5.15pm | Time to greet new customers arriving on an incoming flight. |
| 5.15–5.45pm | Help get all customers onto the coach. Andy does an initial greeting and welcome on the coach during the journey to the resort hotels. |
| 5.45–7.30pm | Drop customers at their hotels. |
| 7.30–8.30pm | Answer any accommodation and check in problems |
| 8.30pm | The end of Andy's day. Time for a well deserved break! |

# EVIDENCE ACTIVITY

## *Lifestyle*

1  In a short, word-processed report describe how a person's lifestyle would be influenced by the jobs they might choose to do. Give specific examples of jobs that you have looked at in this unit, with realistic examples of how the jobs would have both positive and negative effects on the employee.  (M3)

2  Write a brief summary explaining how working in different types of organisations in hospitality, travel and tourism may affect an employee's lifestyle. Choose different types of organisation. For each explain how working for them would impact on an employee's lifestyle.  (D2)

```
A C G W J M
B E Z O K V
S E A R C H
R F I D L O
```

Check your understanding of the information in this unit by answering the following questions. Then find the answers in the wordsearch.

**1** At an airport who is responsible for checking customers onto flights? (8,7,5)

**2** What is the main law that covers hygiene in food handling and production? (4,6,3)

**3** Another term for reception. (5,6)

**4** Industries that do not usually make products but instead provide the public with enjoyable experiences and useful services. (7,10)

**5** Members of food service staff must have good .......... skills? (5)

**6** What is it called when you buy the right to run an outlet of an existing company? (9)

**7** The term used to describe a working day that is divided into more than one session. (11)

**8** This person needs to know about the history of a place. (4,5)

**9** This kind of company operates in more than one country. (13)

**10** What is the term given to a famous product or company? (5)

```
S D B M A F J T T I P E Z X C W S A K C
L E L S O Q F R F O V S N A H F E I T M
J B R L T D T V K H C Y U S E O E D A F
E G U V R F R O L F X S D I F O D H Z G
K O L S I R I A N D C Y T B I D I M V Q
N L D W A C L H B R X S B I P S U C T E
C U S T O M E R S E R V I C E A G E N T
B W D G W N A I Y T F A M T X F R X M Z
M R V O B Z H L N S I U C Z T E U K R B
K W A E K I Y T P D L L M O V T O D I V
N F R N X J R H Q T U V P E Q Y T N W E
D K T Q D U L C I E X S U S U A F P S D
H L D Y I S O N H W G M T C N C J I F Z
A U P G R B A T R E B V L R V T H O T J
Z I M S J T P D N J I S N H I C P K Y B
Q O E C I F F O T N O R F C N E E U P T
W C X O R U Q S Q F K T X A F N S O L G
G R N C G K E O S A H W R M T S A L E S
B A U S Y V A N X U R F R I Y O G L N I
L Y Q E R P L O F N S M E M G E C V J W
```

# unit 2

## Working in hospitality, travel and tourism

In Unit 1 you looked at the huge range of job opportunities that can be found in the hospitality, travel and tourism sector. In this unit you are going to focus on what it actually means to work in the sector. You will investigate what kind of working conditions you might be able to expect and learn about the kinds of procedures that employers usually have in place to introduce new staff to their new job and workplace, and to help them to develop as they continue working in their jobs.

*In this unit you will learn about:*

- ▢ the terms and conditions of different jobs
- ▢ the induction process that new employees go through
- ▢ the procedures that are used for monitoring performance in the workplace.

## Terms and conditions

Unless we are lucky enough to win the lottery, most of us will go to work for a large part of our adult lives. How an **employer** treats you is a key factor in whether you will enjoy your job and want to continue working for the organisation.

> **GLOSSARY**
>
> An **employer** is a person, company or organisation that offers people (employees) work in return for wages.

## GIVE IT A GO: reasons to work

Why would you go to work? Write a list of the reasons that you would go to work for. Consider what you would want and expect to get out of being at work.

There is a good chance that many of you put 'to earn money' at the top of your list! It may surprise you to know that in surveys conducted by employers, while money is important to people, it is not the main reason that most people give for going to work each day.

Over the years there have been many studies examining staff motivation and here are just a few examples of what the research shows employees want from their jobs:

### GLOSSARY

**Environment** means the area and surroundings in which you are working.

- *a good working **environment** – comfortable surroundings, which are not too hot or cold*
- *good working conditions – suitable breaks and reasonable hours*
- *social interaction – being able to meet and socialise with other people*
- *job security – knowing that they are not in danger of suddenly losing their job*
- *the use of their skills or intellect – finding the work interesting*
- *prospects of promotion and a good job title – feeling that their job will develop*
- *responsibility – being allowed to work on their own initiative*
- *recognition and appreciation – praise for achievement*
- *trust and respect – not being treated as a machine*
- *participation in decision making – being involved in decisions not just being told what to do*
- *a sense of belonging – having a chance to get involved and feeling part of company*
- *salary – appropriate pay for the job they are doing*
- *good relationships with management.*

## GIVE IT A GO: reasons why other people work

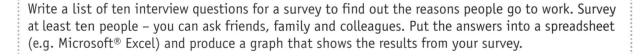

Write a list of ten interview questions for a survey to find out the reasons people go to work. Survey at least ten people – you can ask friends, family and colleagues. Put the answers into a spreadsheet (e.g. Microsoft® Excel) and produce a graph that shows the results from your survey.

People who take jobs in hospitality, travel and tourism may want to travel the world, work in exotic locations and avoid what they see as a nine to five job. The terms and conditions set out the details of the tasks and responsibilities you will be expected to carry out in a job, how much you will be paid and what benefits you may get. You will want to think about these carefully before you decide whether you want to accept a job offer.

## THINK ABOUT IT

Write down what you think might be meant by the words terms and conditions.

## Pay

Terms of employment refers to the conditions with regard to pay and hours worked, in other words how much you will be paid for doing the job and the hours and times that you will be expected to work.

In the past the hospitality, travel and tourism sector has not had a very good reputation for paying high wages and salaries to employees. Nowadays this is changing considerably. As staff are often asked to work unusual hours and because the work is demanding, the sector has found it increasingly difficult to find and keep the right employees. This has meant a steady improvement in the wages, working conditions and benefits being offered by organisations looking to recruit and keep staff.

### GIVE IT A GO: a good starting wage

How much do you think you would want to earn? What do you think would be a good starting wage in hospitality, travel and tourism if you were, for example, a commis chef or a junior sales advisor in a high street travel agency?

£ ?

There are many different methods of payment in operation. It is very important for anyone starting a job to understand how and when they are going to be paid for the work they do. You need to understand the basic information you receive on your pay slips. For example, what is gross pay or net pay? Gross pay is the amount of money you earn before any **deductions** are made, for things such as tax and National Insurance. Net pay is the money you have left after these deductions have been taken out. In other words net pay is the money you actually get each week or month.

### GLOSSARY

**Deductions** are money that is taken out of your pay.

## GIVE IT A GO: terms and conditions

Do you have a part-time job? Write down the terms and conditions that you think you are employed under. If you are not sure, speak to your employers to find out. If you are not working at the moment, ask someone you know about their terms and conditions.

## CASE STUDY – TERMS AND CONDITIONS

Sarah is in charge of a small housekeeping team at a nine-bedroom hotel near Newmarket, Cambridge. She is responsible for the cleanliness of all the guest rooms and the public areas in the hotel. She also has responsibility for the equipment they use.

According to her terms and conditions, Sarah is paid monthly and receives this payment on the last day of each month. Her salary goes straight into her bank account via a bank credit transfer. Sarah's terms and conditions state that she is required to work from 7 am until 2 pm five days a week. She is entitled to an hour's paid break each day. Occasionally Sarah is required to work late or go in over the weekend, for which she receives **time off in lieu**.

### GLOSSARY

**Time off in lieu** is the time that an employee can take off for extra time worked.

Sarah receives a free meal while on duty and a uniform, although she has to wash and maintain it herself. She also benefits from discounts in the hotel restaurant for herself and her immediate family. Sarah has undergone training with the hotel that has included a one-year, part-time course at the local college where she achieved an NVQ Level 1 in Housekeeping. The hotel paid for this training.

**1** Why was it important for Sarah to understand she was going to be paid monthly when she took on her job as housekeeper?

**2** What reasons can you think of why she might occasionally need to work in the evenings or at the weekend?

**3** What benefits does Sarah get?

## GIVE IT A GO: receiving your pay

You may well have a part-time job at the moment. How are you paid for this?

### • *Bank credit transfer (BACS)* •

BACS is one of the most common methods of paying wages and salaries. It stands for bank automated clearing system. This is a computerised system that allows money to be transferred between bank accounts. You may alternatively be paid by cheque or by cash.

## • *Salary or wages?* •

A salaried job pays a fixed amount each year, called a salary, which is divided into equal amounts and paid monthly. Some jobs pay staff hourly instead. This means that if you work for 12 hours in any one week, you get paid for 12 hours. If you are paid weekly on the other hand your terms and conditions may state that you have to work 40 hours. If one week you work for 42 hours, you will still only get paid for 40 hours. However, if the next week you only work 28 hours, you would still be paid for 40.

There are many different ways that people are contracted and paid for the work they do. You might even be contracted short term and only be employed for one, two or three months at a time.

**WHAT if?**

### ... you were paid a salary once a month?

Imagine you moved to a job that pays you your salary once a month when you have been used to being paid every Friday. What are some of the problems you might run into?

## Work patterns

Work patterns refer to how the hours you work are organised. In hospitality, travel and tourism there are many different ways of working. A travel agent working in a high street agency might work regular hours from nine to five, but many posts in the sector, as you have already seen, require irregular or flexible work patterns.

Hospitality, travel and tourism are service industries. This means that the majority of things the sector offers to customers are services, such as flying people to a hotel abroad or providing them with a meal or a drink.

▲ **Cash machines are handy for people who work nine to five**

**WHAT if?**

### ... your hotel did not serve food after 5 pm?

Imagine that you own a small hotel and, to keep all your staff happy, you do not serve any food or drinks after 5 pm. What effect would this have on customers who want a meal or a drink in the evening? What effect would it have on the success of your business?

Companies use the work patterns that allow them to provide services effectively at all the times customers may want them.

## GIVE IT A GO: work patterns

Again, using the example of a small hotel, how might the employers arrange the work patterns of the kitchen staff to ensure that they meet the needs and wants of customers?

### • *Shift patterns* •

There are several patterns of shift working. They usually involve:

- ▭ *working hours that change from time to time*
- ▭ *working hours that may be unsociable*
- ▭ *paying a higher rate for working unsociable hours.*

Some job roles will involve working a night shift. For example, a customer service agent working in one of the UK's major airports may well work unusual and flexible hours, as an airport operates on a 24-hour basis. Night shift workers in airports may be able to work in batches of long hours and then take extended periods of time off, which is sometimes known as 'continental shifts'.

▲ **This woman prefers the day shift**

## WHAT

### *... you worked night shifts as an airport customer service agent?*

Do you think you could cope with getting up at midnight to start your day's work as a customer service agent at 4 am when you were working on night shifts?

There are regulations that control working hours. For example, the Working Time Regulations 1998 aim to stop workers being made to work more than 48 hours per week on average. They also give staff the right to:

- ▭ *one day off each week*
- ▭ *a rest-break of at least 20 minutes if the working day is six hours*
- ▭ *four weeks' paid leave per year and a right to receive holiday pay at the time leave is taken.*

## CASE STUDY – WORKING SPLIT SHIFTS

Tariq works as a chef at the Marlborough Hotel in the Lake District. He enjoys his job very much but the hours are long. A normal day would see him starting work at 10 am. During this shift Tariq would carry out his **mise en place** for the day. All the food needs to be prepared and then at midday the hotel restaurant opens its doors to the day's customers. After a very busy lunchtime service, Tariq then has to ensure that everything is in place for the evening shift. If all goes well, then he will be finished work by 3 pm.

Tariq is back at work at 6 pm for the evening service. As well as cooking all the meals for the hotel's evening customers, Tariq also has to make sure that all of the preparation is completed for the following day. Some preparation can be done the next day but often much of the work needs to be done in advance. For example, the filling for a pie might need to be made the day before so that the final dish can be completed quickly the following day.

If all goes well, he will finish work at 10 pm. This typical day means that Tariq is working for nine hours. There are many other jobs that require staff to work for such long hours but the fact that Tariq is working **split shifts** makes if different from other roles.

### GLOSSARY

**Mise en place** is the preparation undertaken by a chef, such as the washing, peeling and chopping of vegetables before a soup can be made.
**Split shifts** means a working day is divided into two with a break between the shifts.

● What are some of the advantages and disadvantages of working split shifts? Make a list of each and discuss with a partner.

## ● *Flexible working* ●

The hospitality, travel and tourism sector requires a very flexible workforce. Flexitime is one form of flexible working. This is where you are required to work a certain number of hours within a fixed period, but there is some flexibility as to when you complete those hours. In this system you may also be able to arrange time off, if the total number of hours adds up to more than the weekly amount required. This pattern of work tends to be more common in office-based jobs. In hospitality, travel and tourism there may be other informal flexible working. For example, as a tour guide, you might be allowed to decide your own working hours, as long as the job is done and you carry out all your duties.

## ● *Annual leave* ●

All workers have the right to four weeks' paid holiday each year. The nature of the work in this sector may mean that staff are at work when other people are not, including evenings, weekends and holiday periods. This may mean some flexibility is required about when leave is taken. Staff may be asked to take their leave when business is quieter. To many people this might present a problem, but to others it may suit their lifestyle.

### GLOSSARY

**Annual leave** is the paid holiday an employee is entitled to each year.

## Conditions of work

Conditions of work cover a company's voluntary practices and others which are legal requirements.

### ● *Health and safety* ●

Anyone who is working has a right to certain basic conditions, the most important of which is to be able to work in a safe environment. Health and safety are covered by law in the UK. The Health and Safety at Work Act 1974 is the main piece of **legislation** and you will look at this in greater detail in Unit 5.

### ● *Pension rights* ●

What is a pension? A pension is a simple but efficient way of saving for your retirement. The basic state pension is the amount of basic pension you will receive from the government when you reach state pension age. The amount received depends on the number of years in which you have paid National Insurance contributions.

Many people also set up personal pension schemes to try to ensure they have enough money to live on when they retire. Anyone under the age of 75 can contribute to a pension scheme. Some employers operate a pension scheme for their staff. The amount you get in these schemes usually depends on the number of years you have been a member of the scheme and your earnings on retirement.

Nearly all employers must offer their employees access to a pension scheme called a stakeholder pension. The employer does not have to make a contribution but many choose to do so.

### ● *Health schemes* ●

Employees who work for a major company, such as the InterContinental Hotels Group, might benefit from a private health scheme. These schemes offer free medical treatment, such as consultations with doctors and operations.

## Benefits

As well as receiving wages, many jobs provide employees with other benefits. These might include cash bonuses for excellent work or at certain busy times of the year, such as over the Christmas period. Chefs and waiting staff may well receive meals on duty or free uniforms. Many airline staff receive free or discounted flights. Hotel staff might be free to make use of facilities at their hotels, such as the gym. Staff at a tourist attraction might receive free tickets for themselves or family members. Staff working at an airport such as Heathrow in London might receive interest-free loans to help with the purchase of travel season tickets.

## GIVE IT A GO: employment benefits

1 Working with a colleague think about the following list of benefits an employee might receive. Write a description of what you and your partner understand by each benefit. Then decide in which industry staff might receive the benefits. Are they likely to be received by employees working in hospitality, travel or tourism – or all three industries?

- bonuses
- meals on duty
- use of facilities
- free transport
- luncheon vouchers
- season ticket loans
- information on special offers
- discounts
- free entry to attractions.

2 Produce an eye-catching poster that could be displayed at a recruitment fair. It should clearly identify some of the possible benefits to anyone thinking of working in the hospitality, travel and tourism sector.

## EVIDENCE ACTIVITY  P1  M1

### Identifying and comparing terms and conditions

1 Identify three different job advertisements for work that you think might suit somebody just starting out in hospitality, travel and tourism. Look in local newspapers and **trade journals** such as *Caterer & Hotelkeeper* or *Travel Weekly* – your tutor will be able to help you find these.

2 Make a list of the terms and conditions being offered. For example, how much are they offering to pay?

3 Compare the terms and conditions being offered for each of these jobs.

4 Produce a table that shows the similarities and differences between each of the offers of employment.

> **GLOSSARY**
>
> **A trade journal** is a magazine that is published for people working in a specific industry, usually monthly.

▲ Trade journals can be a good place to job hunt

# The induction process

## The people

All businesses and organisations should ensure that new staff go through what is called an induction process. This simply means showing new members of staff all of the important things that they will need to know in order to work effectively in the organisation.

**WHAT if?**

### ... *you were starting a new job as a visitor attraction guide?*

Imagine arriving for your first day at work as a visitor attraction guide at Alton Towers. If you were thrown straight into the job without any guidance, what problems could this cause for you and the company?

The induction process helps staff settle into their job roles quickly and effectively. A good induction process helps a person feel part of the team. It will also bring other benefits to the organisation, such as improved customer satisfaction. Staff will be more effective in what they are doing and so customers will get better service. An organisation's reputation will improve, as customers will see that the staff are well trained. An effective induction process is also vital in terms of ensuring high standards of health and safety.

**GIVE IT A GO: starting work in a bar**

If you were starting work as a member of the bar staff in a busy city centre bar, what do you think you would need to know before you began work? Create a table similar to the one below and draw up a list. Say why you think that these things would be important.

| Things the induction needs to cover | Why it is important |
|---|---|
|  |  |
|  |  |

### ● *Who to report to* ●

During an effective induction any new member of staff should be shown or told who they are reporting to – in other words who their supervisor or boss is. It may be the supervisor's responsibility to make sure that all aspects of the induction are carried out.

### ● *Expected behaviour and uniform* ●

New staff will also need to know what is expected behaviour while on duty, including what clothes or uniform they should wear. This will often be set out in a company's **code of conduct**.

### ● *Absence from work* ●

The induction process should also cover procedures related to absence from work. These include:

- ▷ *what the new member of staff must do if they cannot come into work because of sickness*
- ▷ *arranging annual leave*
- ▷ *other situations that need special leave, such as **bereavement**.*

### ● *Training* ●

Any training new members of staff may need will also be identified during induction. You will look at this issue more closely later in the unit.

## The organisation

As part of the induction process, it is important for a new member of staff to learn about the organisation they are now working for. Understanding the aims of an organisation and how it works can help make new members of staff feel more involved and help them to settle in to their new role.

### ● *Organisational structure* ●

All businesses have to organise what they do. There are many ways to structure a business. A company is often structured by function, which means arranging the business according to what each department does. For example, a large travel and tourism organisation might be structured so that separate departments look after the following areas:

- ▷ *Human Resources – looking after all issues concerning the staff*
- ▷ *Sales and Marketing – advertising and selling the products and services*
- ▷ *Research and Development – looking at new products and services*
- ▷ *Production/Operations – actually running and providing the products and services*
- ▷ *Customer Service – looking after the customers*

> **GLOSSARY**
>
> **A code of conduct** explains how any employee must behave and act while at work.

> **GLOSSARY**
>
> **Bereavement** is the death of someone close.

🖙 *Finance and Accounts – handling all of the issues concerning money*
🖙 *Administration and IT – providing support to other departments.*

Organisations need to develop a structure that best suits their own needs and purposes.

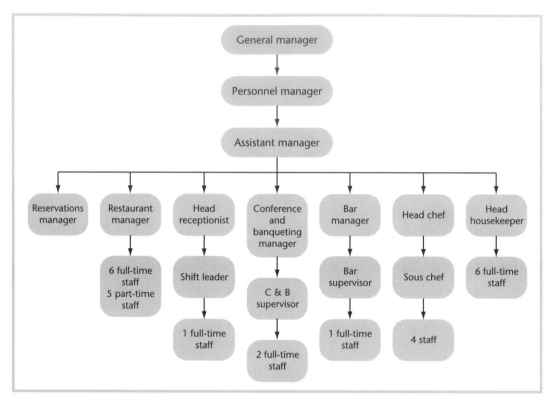

▲ The organisational structure of a hotel might look like this

## ● *Statutory regulations* ●

By law all organisations are required to make sure that certain basic conditions exist in a workplace. These important areas are shown in the spider diagram below.

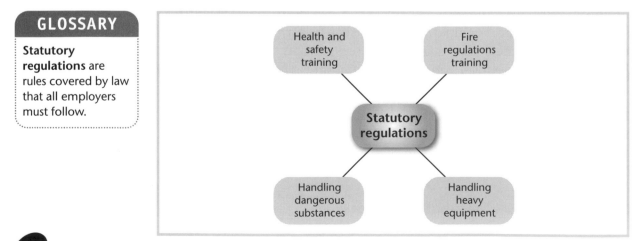

### GLOSSARY

**Statutory regulations** are rules covered by law that all employers must follow.

These are areas that any new members of staff must be told about as soon as they start a new job. For example, an employee working on the housekeeping staff will have to use cleaning materials, many of which contain dangerous substances. These can be a hazard if not used properly and so it is vital that all new staff have the correct training before they use them.

## GIVE IT A GO: hazards at work

Do you know these symbols? They are all hazards you might meet at work. Working with a partner, try to find out what each one means.

## Documents

### • *Contract of employment* •

During induction new members of staff should also receive any relevant paperwork or documentation. This might include a contract of employment. This contract is a written agreement between the employer and employee that states the agreed terms and conditions of employment. Some part-time jobs may not have written contracts.

### • *Staff handbook* •

Many companies also give out staff handbooks to new staff. These usually include the company's code of conduct and details of procedures, such as basic hygiene rules. The staff handbook is a written record of all the things that staff need to know to help them in their job. After all, there is a lot to remember for anyone starting a new job.

## EVIDENCE ACTIVITY — D1

### *How can induction help?*

Explain how an effective induction process can be used to help any new member of staff to understand the terms and conditions of his or her new job.

EVIDENCE ACTIVITY

## *Induction*

Within your local area, identify one organisation that operates in the hospitality, travel and tourism sector. Contact the company and find out how they approach induction of new staff. Ask them if they can provide you with information on their induction procedures. It may be better if this is done with the use of a formal letter. Report back on your findings. Write a short summary of what you found in the form of a word-processed document. Make sure you include the following.

1  Describe the purpose of an induction process.  **(P2)**

2  Use your research to explain how the company you have contacted uses induction **(P3)** to help its staff settle into their job roles quickly and effectively.

3  Explain why induction is so important to organisations and individuals.  **(M2)**

# Procedures

## Staff development

When you are offered a job in the hospitality, travel and tourism sector, it is because the organisation offering you the job believes that you will be suitable for the role. Most new members of staff will need some training in order to be able to do their new job. Equipment and products are different from company to company, which means that staff with experience also need training. Even the most talented new member of staff will need support and guidance to do the job well.

Staff development is the term used to describe the on-the-job training and support that companies can offer to all staff, new and old, to help them get better at their work and also to enjoy the jobs they are doing more.

WHAT **if?**

### *... you worked as a customer service agent?*

Imagine that you are working at London Luton Airport as a customer service agent for easyJet. Write a list of the activities that you would do every day that would be new to you in this role. How could your employers help you to do them better?

## ● *Skills development* ●

While all employees will have certain skills already, good employers can help their staff develop their skills to the advantage of all concerned.

Someone working in a hotel gym might already be very fit and possess a lot of agility and stamina, but they may not have had much experience of dealing with members of the public. All of us have different skills levels, but they can be improved.

Skills that staff may need development and training in include:

- *working with others – for example, working in a bar involves working in a team with other staff*
- *practical aspects of how to use equipment – for example, using the telephones or operating the till*
- *specific techniques – for example, a barperson in a busy city centre pub may need to learn how to make and serve a wide variety of drinks and cocktails, or how to change a barrel of beer*
- *specific areas of knowledge – for example, a guide at a cathedral in Staffordshire would need to know the history of the building and surrounding area in great detail*
- *knowledge of the law – for example, the legislation covering the sale of alcohol or food safety.*

▲ A barperson may need to learn how to serve a variety of cocktails

## • *Mentoring* •

Mentoring is used by some organisations as a way to help staff develop. This is where someone more experienced guides a new member of staff.

# Staff appraisals

Nowadays many companies use staff appraisals to monitor performance and assess the progress of their staff. These appraisals are designed to help the organisation get the best out of all of their employees. They are also vital in helping to keep and develop staff and to raise an organisation's profile and reputation as the case study below shows.

## CASE STUDY – LONDON MARRIOTT HOTEL, REGENTS PARK

We invest a great deal of time and money into training our staff to be the best they can be. In the hotel and catering industry, providing first-class service to guests is one of the most important aspects of the job. If staff are not trained to provide this service well, guests will stay elsewhere. It's as simple as that.

At the London Marriott Hotel, Regents Park, its 200 staff are given rigorous training in the art of customer care. The London Marriott Hotel, Regents Park, believes it has created an environment where both staff and guests are satisfied. Andrew Currie explains: 'The Marriott's culture is "If you look after your staff, they will look after your customers" and this is something we strongly believe in. Through our training and staff development programmes staff are encouraged to seek promotion and we always try to promote from within. If staff are satisfied, they will stay with us for longer.'

All operational staff, from chambermaids and concierge through to receptionists and chefs, are given a three-month training programme, which Andrew Currie believes gives them the confidence to do their jobs well. 'Our staff are our most important asset and we aim to keep them motivated and enthusiastic.'

Source:
www.mattison.co.uk/pressreleases/focus/London Marriott Hotel.PDF

1 Why do you think the London Marriott Hotel has been able to reduce its staff turnover rate to 40%?

2 What message will the fact that the hotel has achieved an Investors in People Award send out to anyone who might be considering working there?

3 Why does the organisation place so much importance on its *operational* staff?

Appraisals also help the staff get the most from the jobs they are doing. They are a chance for you as an employee to:

🗩 *talk to your employer about how you are progressing*
🗩 *ask for any support you would like in developing your skills*
🗩 *say how you would like to develop your career.*

## GIVE IT A GO: having an appraisal

Talk to your friends and family who are working. Have they been appraised? Is their work and performance monitored? If it is, ask them how and whether they find it useful.

### • *Aims and objectives* •

If an appraisal is going to be effective for both the employer and the employee, it must be carefully planned. The employee needs to know the **aims** and **objectives** beforehand. The employee may use a pre-appraisal questionnaire to prepare. If you have a **job description**, this will usually provide the **criteria** for the appraisal.

The following **agenda** for an appraisal shows how a typical appraisal might be carried out.

**1** Talk through the pre-appraisal questionnaire first.

**2** Discuss the **appraisee's** performance against the objectives on the appraisal form.

**3** Discuss the appraisee's abilities or skills.

**4** Identify development needs and start to complete the plan.

**5** Agree overall assessment.

**6** Discuss and agree goals for next year.

**7** Agree follow-up action and review dates.

▲ **Learning the art of pastry making**

If the aim for a young chef was to eventually take control of the pastry section of the kitchen, some objectives might be to learn and perfect four or five different types of pastry, to master a variety of sweets and desserts and to learn to work with and use chocolate in cooking. All of these smaller step objectives, once achieved will allow the chef to progress to the overall aim of taking charge of the entire pastry section.

### • *Recording outcomes* •

If the employer and the employee are to benefit from the use of an appraisal

> **GLOSSARY**
>
> **Aims** are the overall things that are to be achieved.
> **Objectives** are the smaller steps that will be undertaken to help achieve the overall aims.
> A **job description** sets out the tasks and activities that a person does in their job role.
> **Criteria** are the standards by which a person is assessed.

> **GLOSSARY**
>
> An **agenda** is a list of things to be dealt with.

> **GLOSSARY**
>
> **Appraisee** is the person who is being appraised.

45

system, the outcomes of the appraisal need to be recorded and documented. This record has two purposes:

- *members of staff know what is expected of them and where they might be able to progress to*
- *the organisation has a record of the training and support that will help them get the best out of their employees.*

## EVIDENCE ACTIVITY — P4 P5 M3

### *Procedures for monitoring performance*

1 Produce a form, using your IT skills, that could be used to help a manager or supervisor in hospitality, travel and tourism to monitor the performance of a new member of staff in one of the roles you have looked at. Prepare a set of notes to go with the form that:

- describe how you would monitor an employee's work and how you would use the form **P5**

- say why it is important that work is monitored. **P4**

2 Give three examples of how work procedures are used to monitor individual performance. If possible use real examples of how work procedures are used to monitor individual staff performance in companies that you have studied or worked in. **M3**

## EVIDENCE ACTIVITY — D2

### *Importance of monitoring performance*

Why is performance monitoring important to:

- the employer
- the employee
- the customer?

---

**GLOSSARY**

**Disciplinary procedures** are the policies a company has in place to ensure problems are dealt with fairly.

## Disciplinary and grievance procedures

Occasionally there are problems at work. It might be that the company is unhappy with the behaviour or actions of an employee or the organisation does not think a member of staff is doing his or her job properly. If an action is not serious, it will probably be dealt with informally. If the problem continues over a period of time or is serious, it is likely to lead to disciplinary procedures against the person. Disciplinary procedures usually follow these stages:

1  a verbal warning is given (the employee is told that he or she is doing or has done something wrong)

2  if it happens again or no improvement is made, a written warning might be needed

3  a final written warning is given

4  only after this process has been carried out can the employee be dismissed.

There will be times when the problem is the other way around and an individual member of staff is unhappy at the way he or she is being treated. Employees can try to solve the problem by following the company's grievance procedures. This also follows a laid-down process:

1  the organisation tries to address the employee's **grievance** informally

2  if this is not possible the employee might need to put his or her concerns in writing to a manager

3  if the problem is still not solved, the employee can go to a more senior manager.

An employee who is facing disciplinary or grievance procedures can get advice and help from a union.

**GLOSSARY**

**Grievance** is when an employee is unhappy about something they are being asked to do at work, or about the conditions they are working in, or the way they are being treated at work.

## THINK ABOUT IT

Working with a partner make a list of the possible situations in hospitality, travel and tourism that could occur that might cause an employee to have a grievance against their employer.

### ● *Sources of advice* ●

There are several organisations that can help companies and individuals solve disputes that arise in the workplace. An individual employee might go to the Citizens Advice Bureau (CAB) to get advice. The Hotel & Catering International Management Association (HCIMA) is a professional body for managers and potential managers in the hospitality industry. It too can offer advice and support to both individuals and the industry. Employees with a valid grievance might go to an industrial tribunal. This is an independent panel set up to make decisions when there is a serious dispute or an employee believes he or she has been treated unfairly.

In a major dispute the employees as a group may be involved. If the employer and the employees cannot agree on a solution, they may go to an organisation called the Advisory, Conciliation and Arbitration Service, known as ACAS. This organisation will listen carefully to both sides in any dispute and then make a decision that everyone involved must agree to follow.

# Termination

## • *Redundancy* •

Every now and then people may find that the original job that they were employed to do is changing from the one that was originally agreed. This is known as job restructuring. In some cases this may mean that certain job roles will no longer exist and staff may face redundancy. This means your contract and employment is ended by the employer, but with payment to make up for the loss of the work. For example, an employee might receive a month's pay for every year they have been with the company. In all these situations there is strict law in the UK to protect employees from simply being sacked or having their job changed from the one they were contracted to do. If an organisation wants or needs to make changes to people's working conditions and contracts, they must follow clearly laid-down procedures.

## • *Dismissal* •

If an employee commits an act of gross misconduct, he or she may be dismissed. This is where employees break the trust and confidence that the employer has in them. Examples would be theft, fighting or assault, being unable to do your job as a result of drinking too much alcohol or being under the influence of illegal drugs, and serious **negligence** which causes unacceptable damage or injury.

### 🗨 THINK ABOUT IT

How would you feel if you knew that any day you could be told that you were no longer needed at work and that you had lost your job?

## • *Resignation* •

When you decide that you no longer want to work for a company, you must hand in your notice to leave the organisation. Resignation procedures will be set out in the staff handbook. The main reason for people leaving their job is because they are moving on to another job. It may be that the new job has better pay, better hours or is in a better location. They may feel that they have learned all they can in their current job and need to find a new challenge. There are lots of opportunities to move around both in terms of location and the type of job within the hospitality, travel and tourism sector.

▲ **Moving on to new challenges**

Check your understanding of the information in this unit by answering the following questions. Then find the answers in the wordsearch.

**1** What is the person who provides a job called? (8)

**2** A trainee chef is often called a ......................... (6)

**3** The term for a job where you are paid a set amount each month or year. (8)

**4** What is it called if you are able to decide the hours that you work yourself? (9)

**5** The short name of the law that protects employee's health and safety while they are working. (6)

**6** A benefit that some staff working in hospitality or travel and tourism might receive. (4, 8)

**7** This document informs staff how they should act at work. (4, 2, 7)

**8** Staff ......................... is very important for all employees. (11)

**9** What is it called when the work and performance of staff are reviewed? (9)

**10** What term is used to describe the situation when a person is no longer needed at work or the job no longer exists? (10)

| F | G | F | S | R | F | I | K | P | P | H | S | Q | A | T |
|---|---|---|---|---|---|---|---|---|---|---|---|---|---|---|
| V | K | L | I | R | E | Y | O | L | P | M | E | P | M | C |
| H | J | E | M | U | P | D | E | E | R | D | P | S | A | U |
| Y | A | X | M | H | C | K | U | O | B | R | K | W | L | D |
| D | J | I | O | F | T | B | F | N | A | U | A | M | V | N |
| N | E | T | C | T | X | I | U | I | D | S | J | H | C | O |
| A | L | I | Y | Y | N | F | S | W | A | A | W | P | G | C |
| A | B | M | R | U | P | A | U | H | Y | W | N | L | U | F |
| V | V | E | E | A | L | B | M | Z | P | C | N | C | S | O |
| H | D | E | V | E | L | O | P | M | E | N | T | W | Y | E |
| G | R | X | W | V | L | A | H | C | K | F | Q | J | X | D |
| F | C | K | D | O | K | P | S | H | G | B | S | A | A | O |
| F | G | T | A | O | C | O | X | T | O | K | Z | X | G | C |
| F | E | P | N | S | Y | X | B | S | H | A | Q | R | L | N |
| G | L | L | R | L | H | E | G | V | B | K | C | Y | X | K |

# unit 3

## Introducing customer service

This unit introduces you to the basic aspects of customer service, including different types of customer and their differing needs and expectations. Good communication is vital to many situations, especially customer service. As you have seen in Units 1 and 2, customer service has a central role in hospitality, travel and tourism. You will find out about the importance of good communication skills within customer service. You will have opportunities to develop these skills and to demonstrate them in practice.

First impressions count and can be crucial to delivering good customer service. You will also develop your understanding of how important it is to create a positive impression of yourself and the organisation you represent.

*In this unit you will learn about:*

⇨ different types of customer and their needs and expectations
⇨ how you can prepare yourself and your work area for customer service
⇨ how to demonstrate good communication skills
⇨ how to provide good care and service to your customer.

# Different types of customer

Hospitality, travel and tourism organisations offer a huge variety of products and services to many different customers. In this section you will think about the different kinds of customer you will meet.

## External customers

When we say customers we are generally referring to those customers who actually buy or use an organisation's products and services. These customers are external customers. For example:

- ▢ *a family booking a two-week holiday to Majorca in a travel agency*
- ▢ *an overseas visitor requesting information in the tourist information centre of the city that he has just arrived in*
- ▢ *a guest staying at a hotel*
- ▢ *an airline passenger flying from London to Paris*
- ▢ *a business man flying to New York and staying in a hotel for three nights.*

## GIVE IT A GO: different types of customer

Look at the external customers in the picture. What different types of customer do you see?

Some of the main groups of external customers are as follows:

- **Business customers** – *travelling on behalf of their company, for example attending a conference*
- **Private customers** – *travelling on holiday or to visit friends and relatives, choosing how and when to travel in their own free time*
- **Groups** – *people who decide to travel together. Sometimes discounts are available if a group of people travel together on the same holiday*
- **Overseas customers/different nationalities** – *visitors from other countries taking a holiday in the UK*
- **Domestic customers** – *people who live in the UK choosing to take a holiday in the UK. For example, someone living in Newcastle may choose to take a holiday in Cornwall*
- **Young children** – *generally children aged under 10 years, who may require additional help and assistance*
- **Elderly** – *people in their 70s and 80s who enjoy travelling, who may require additional help*
- **Disabled** – *passengers who use a wheelchair, for example, may require extra help boarding an aircraft*
- **Emotional needs** – *for example an angry/confused person who requires someone to be calm and patient.*

## Internal customers

Internal customers are members of staff within an organisation or outside suppliers who help us provide the service to external customers. The people you work with are your customers too because you are also in a service relationship with them. You can help them provide the best product or service for their customers and they can help you serve your customers by finding out information for each other and sharing ideas and knowledge. Outside suppliers are important to you in the same way. For example, the brochure delivery man bringing brochures to the travel agency helps the staff to sell holidays to their customers.

Internal customers include:

- **Colleagues** – *people that you work with directly and who have a similar status to you*
- **Managers and supervisors** – *most employees have a direct line manager in the organisation, either a supervisor, head of department or manager*
- **Staff teams** – *groups of staff who form a team to undertake specific functions or jobs. For example, a tourist attraction may have a health and safety team made up of staff from different departments and many hotels have a fire evacuation team that works together to evacuate the building if the fire alarm sounds*
- **Employees** – *if you are self-employed or own a company, you may employ people to work for your organisation*

▭ *Staff in other departments* – people who do not work directly with you, but contribute to the job that you do. For example, the personnel, finance and marketing departments in a large hotel chain will help the staff in each hotel location do their job better

▭ *Contractors* – people who have a short-term job contract with an organisation to complete a specific job, for example an overseas tour guide who has a contract to escort a 14-day tour in Canada during June, July and August only.

## GIVE IT A GO: internal and external customers

Imagine that you work as a travel sales consultant in a busy travel agency. Look at the list of different customers in the table below and identify whether each customer is an internal or an external customer to you. Copy the table and put a tick in the correct column.

| Customer | Internal | External |
|---|---|---|
| A businessman booking a room in a four-star hotel | | |
| A van driver delivering brochures | | |
| The cashier giving you change for your customer | | |
| A lady asking for brochures about a city break to New York | | |
| Two students asking for brochures on Cyprus for an assignment | | |
| A computer engineer installing a new system | | |
| The manager explaining to you how to make a car hire reservation | | |

Now compare your answers with a partner. Discuss any situations where you have ticked different columns and come to an answer that you both agree on.

## Customer needs

Every customer has a different need. Some customers may want to buy goods, such as souvenirs at a visitor attraction or pay for a service, for example waiter service in a restaurant rather than a buffet. Some may require information, for example asking for directions to a museum. Some may have a specific enquiry: 'What is the temperature like in Singapore in September?' Many customers have similar **routine** needs, that is things that are needed frequently. For example in a bus station a frequently asked question may be 'How regular is the coach service from here to Manchester?' There will be other customers who have non-routine needs, such as someone with a food allergy eating in a restaurant. Some people may have special needs. For example, a **visually impaired** customer may not be able to read departure boards at stations and airports and therefore needs announcements to be made.

> **GLOSSARY**
>
> **Routine** is something done the same way every time or that has a regular procedure.
> **Visually impaired** means someone who has some loss of sight.

## GIVE IT A GO: customer needs

1 Match each type of customer to a need that they may have.

| | |
|---|---|
| Elderly man | A lively resort with lots of bars |
| Young family | A hotel with entertainment most evenings |
| Group of girls, aged 20–24 | Access to the Internet at the airport |
| Business man | A resort without hills or steep steps |
| Lady using a wheelchair | A hotel with children's clubs |
| Single person travelling alone | Tourist information in a foreign language |
| Overseas visitor in England | Lifts, ramps and slopes in accommodation and resort |

2 In pairs, take a trip around your school or college. One of you must act as a customer with a non-routine or special need, such as a visually impaired person, a wheelchair user, a parent with a young child in a pram. The second person will act as an escort. Report back on your experiences and present your findings to your tutor and the rest of your class. Your report should include:

- how easy it was to negotiate your way round
- which paths you were unable to take
- how easy/difficult the doors were to open and close
- how easy the lifts were to find and operate
- how many of the stairs or steps had a ramp for alternative use.

# Customer expectations

Customers have **expectations**. This means that when they come to your organisation they have a sense of how they would like to be treated. They want to know that they will get good customer service and

> **GLOSSARY**
>
> **Expectations** are what an individual thinks will happen in a specific situation.

care from staff. After all they are paying! Staff in customer service need to be skilled to meet customers' expectations. This involves:

- ▷ *creating the right impression*
- ▷ *giving customers prompt attention*
- ▷ *good communication skills.*

### • *The right impression* •

When we visit an organisation and meet an employee for the first time, we have expectations. For example, we would expect certain standards of cleanliness, such as employees to be wearing clean and ironed uniforms. We would expect employees' hair to be neat and tidy and for them to greet us in a welcoming and friendly way. We would also expect the premises to be tidy with suitable desks, chairs and equipment for both staff and customers. The impression that we get on visiting the organisation will help us decide whether to stay and ask for information or even make a purchase.

## GIVE IT A GO: the right impression

Study the two pictures below and list their differences.

- What is your first impression of each travel agency area?
- Which travel agency would you prefer to book your holiday at?
- What do you think the impression tells you about the person and the organisation?

## ● *Prompt attention* ●

It is also important to provide prompt attention and to welcome and help customers when they visit your company or organisation. You may walk into an organisation and find there are no staff to help, they are on the phone or they ignore you while they complete paperwork. Alternatively, a very enthusiastic person may approach you as soon as you enter the organisation and bombard you with questions before you are ready to talk to them. Getting the balance right can be difficult, but it does get easier with experience.

### CASE STUDY – GOOD CUSTOMER SERVICE?

Mrs Akram could not decide exactly where to go for her next holiday, so she decided to visit her local travel agent to get information and brochures. She walked into the travel agent; it was bright and cheerful with many brochures on display. There were three members of staff sitting at their desks. None was with a customer.

**Situation 1**  Mrs Akram walked up and down the brochure rack. There were so many! How could she choose? She looked across at the three staff. All had their heads down and looked busy with paperwork. She decided to take some brochures home for inspiration. She collected a pile of brochures and left.

**Situation 2**  A few seconds after Mrs Akram entered, one of the agents jumped up and walked quickly round to help. She asked a few questions to get an idea of what Mrs Akram wanted. She recommended three brochures that had the sort of holiday Mrs Akram liked. She gave her a business card and invited Mrs Akram to return when she had looked at the brochures with her husband.

- How do you think Mrs Akram would have felt on each occasion?
- Which situation is best? Discuss the reasons why with a partner.

## EVIDENCE ACTIVITY

### *Needs and expectations*

Visit a local travel and tourism organisation, such as a travel agency, museum or tourist information centre. Observe the different types of customers who visit the organisation. Write a short report that identifies at least three different types of customer who use that organisation and describe their individual needs and expectations.

## ● *Good communication* ●

Good communication is vital to providing good customer service.

## GIVE IT A GO: communication skills

Mario went in to a travel agency to get some information about Crete. Here is the conversation he had with a sales consultant:

| | |
|---|---|
| Mario: | Hello! I'd like some information on Crete. |
| Sales Consultant: | Uh-huh? |
| Mario: | Can you tell me what the temperature is like in June and what the prices are for a two-week holiday? |
| Sales Consultant: | Um ... I'll try and find a brochure. *A short while later*. This is an OK brochure. |
| Mario: | Thank you. I'll have a good look at this at home. |

What could the sales consultant have said to improve her communication with Mario? Rewrite the scenario to make the communication from the sales consultant more positive.

# Prepare yourself and your work area

Good preparation helps you do your job better. For example, if you have a message pad and a pen beside the telephone, you are able to write down the customers' details immediately and by doing this you will demonstrate excellent customer service.

## Prepare yourself

### • *Personal presentation* •

Our first impression of the staff in an organisation will influence our decision about whether to stay and buy a product. For example, a hotel receptionist looking smart will encourage customers to stay at the hotel.

Many jobs in the hospitality, travel and tourism sector require employees to wear a uniform. Different types of uniform are worn for different roles, for example:

- *travel agent*
- *air cabin crew*
- *resort representative*
- *children's representative*
- *waiter*
- *hotel receptionist*
- *chef.*

## GIVE IT A GO: wearing a uniform

Describe the type of uniform each role in the list above wears. What are the advantages of the uniform for each role?

It is also important to have regulations about how the uniform is worn. For example, it should be clean and ironed at all times.

## EVIDENCE ACTIVITY

### Design a uniform

1   Look in travel trade journals and magazines, such as the *Travel Trade Gazette*, *Travel Weekly*, *Caterer & Hotelkeeper*, to collect examples of the variety of uniforms worn in the industry.

2   Working in small groups, choose one job in the hospitality and travel industries and design a uniform for employees to wear. Use catalogues such as *Additions* or *Freemans* to cut out the items and calculate the cost of providing the uniform to each member of staff. Remember that staff working full time may need more than one set of clothes.

3   Discuss with the whole class the various standards and types of uniform worn and why they are different for different jobs.

4   Why is it important to present yourself appropriately for work in a customer service environment?

## • *Posture* •

Your posture is another important part of creating the right first impression. Employees should be proud to represent their company and they should stand upright and appear confident and enthusiastic.

## • *Personal space* •

Most people do not like it if, when they meet someone for the first time, that person stands too close. Everyone has an invisible boundary around their body which they do not like other people to cross (apart from our family and people we love). This is called your personal space. It is important to make sure that you do not make your customers feel uncomfortable in this way. After all, making customers feel comfortable is a big part of the customer service role!

> **GLOSSARY**
>
> **Posture** is the way people hold their bodies when they are standing up or sitting down.

## WHAT  if?

### ... you were at a party and someone entered your personal space?

Imagine you are at a party and you meet someone for the first time. This person stands really close to you all evening and seems to follow you around the party. How do you feel?

## • Positive attitude •

When dealing with customers it is always good to have a positive attitude. The way you say and do things has a direct impact on others around you, especially your customers.

## CASE STUDY – I HATE MONDAYS!

Alison works in a travel agency and hates Monday mornings. She finds it especially difficult to get out of bed on Mondays and the bus journey is always longer than on other days. Today the bus was ten minutes late. She scowled at the driver when she got on and when she got off the bus at the stop near her work.

Sasha let her in the shop with a smile and a cheerful 'Morning! Did you have a good weekend?' Alison grunted a greeting and rushed past her towards the staff room, where she made herself a coffee. She had only had a few sips, when the manager ushered everyone to their desks, ready to serve customers. Alison sat at the desk furthest away from the door. When the day's tasks were allocated, Alison was asked to update and change the window cards. 'Why me?' thought Alison, 'I did this on Friday afternoon.'

- Write the words and phrases where Alison's negative attitude is shown.
- How might Alison's life change if she had a positive attitude?
- On a separate piece of paper rewrite the scenario, so that Alison acts positively.
- Work in two groups. Act out the negative and then a positive scenario that your whole group agrees on.

## • Knowledge of organisation's products or services •

It is important to know about the products and services your organisation offers so you can make suggestions to customers and find the best product to meet their needs. The induction process, as you saw in Unit 2, will include training on an organisation's products or services.

## • Knowledge of organisation's guidelines and standards •

Every organisation has its own **guidelines** and standards that staff must follow, to ensure that the same high standard of customer service is

### GLOSSARY

**Guidelines** are standard procedures to follow.

provided to every customer. It is vital that staff work together and demonstrate positive teamwork to help each other help the customer.

## • *Teamwork* •

When we are at work we have certain responsibilities and duties that we need to take care of correctly and in the time available. Some jobs can be completed more quickly and more efficiently when we work with other people. For example, a hotel receptionist might help a colleague check in a large group of people who have all arrived at the same time. When colleagues help each other to do their work and improve the service provided to customers, it is known as teamwork.

### GIVE IT A GO: teamwork

Read the case study on page 60 again. How good a team member was Alison? How do you think Alison's colleagues and manager feel about working with her?

## Prepare your work area

It is important that your work area is safe and tidy and that it meets health and safety standards. It should be designed so that there is efficient use of space and to ensure that accidents rarely happen.

## EVIDENCE ACTITIVY 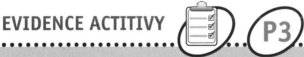 P3

### *Your work area*

1 Identify areas of concern in the picture of a work area.

2 Discuss with a partner what changes you would make.

3 Describe what makes a good work area for an employee to provide excellent customer service.

Organisations must ensure that they provide the correct equipment to deal with fires.

# Communication skills

Good communication is vital to providing good customer service. When things go wrong, they often happen due to poor communication. In this section you will look at how to develop these skills.

## Different types of communications

It is important to choose the most appropriate way to communicate with both external and internal customers. We can communicate in a number of ways.

**Internet** – the Internet is a telephone/computer system allowing communication around the world and is used to contact external customers.

**Intranet** – an Intranet is similar to the Internet but is used inside an organisation only.

**Email** – this is an electronic way of sending written communication and may be more informal than writing by letter.

**Letter** – this is a formal method of written business communication. There are standards of presentation and layout that should be used to give the right impression to your customers.

**Verbal communication** – this occurs when we speak to our customers face to face or by telephone. This is a good way to communicate with customers when we require an immediate response.

### ⬭ THINK ABOUT IT

Confidential information is information that is private and should only be exchanged between you and the customer concerned. Which communication methods are appropriate when passing on confidential information?

## Skills

We can improve our own communication skills by practising and by listening and watching our successful colleagues.

### ● *Appropriate language* ●

It is important to use appropriate language when you speak to, or write to, your customers. The words you use when speaking to your friends are often different to those you use when serving customers at work.

## GIVE IT A GO: language!

Look at the sentences below, which may be spoken to friends, and rewrite them to be more appropriate when helping customers.

Hiya!

You what?

See ya!

No, that's not right …

Just as with speaking, when you are communicating in writing you need to make sure that you are using appropriate language. With friends you use more informal language. When texting to friends you may also shorten or misspell words to make your message short. However, when writing to both internal and external customers you need to give a professional image at all times. Therefore, it is important to ensure that you use proper words and check that your spelling and grammar are correct. A typed letter gives a more positive and professional image than one that is hand written.

## GIVE IT A GO: written communication

Here is a letter that a new member of staff at a three-star hotel was going to send to a customer.

1 Identify the spelling and grammar mistakes.

2 Rewrite and word-process the letter to give the best possible impression. Include any extra information that you believe would make the letter more professional and welcoming.

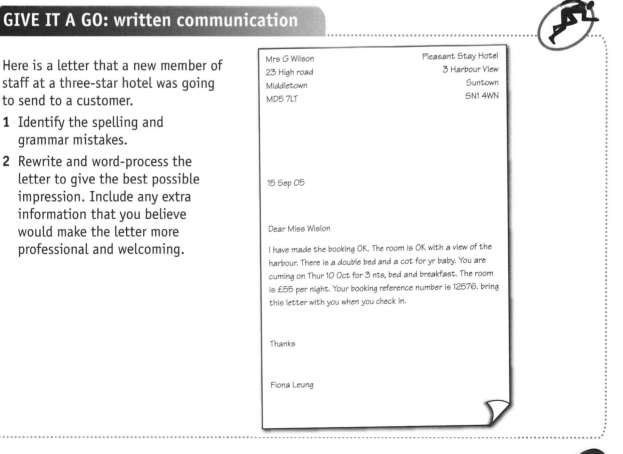

Mrs G Wilson
23 High road
Middletown
MD5 7LT

Pleasant Stay Hotel
3 Harbour View
Suntown
SN1 4WN

15 Sep 05

Dear Miss Wislon

I have made the booking OK. The room is OK with a view of the harbour. There is a double bed and a cot for yr baby. You are cuming on Thur 10 Oct for 3 nts, bed and breakfast. The room is £55 per night. Your booking reference number is 12576. bring this letter with you when you check in.

Thanks

Fiona Leung

## • *Level and tone of voice* •

It is not just what you say that is important, but also how you say it. You want to build **rapport** and trust with customers so they feel good about you and will want to buy your product or service. The level and tone of your voice can give as strong a message as the actual words you say.

### GIVE IT A GO: verbal communication

In pairs, practise saying the following sentence in different tones of voice so that you communicate the feelings listed below. Then say them out loud for the other groups to guess how you are feeling.

'Good morning! How may I help you?'

| | | | |
|---|---|---|---|
| happy | bored | angry | enthusiastic |
| uninterested | tired | sad | couldn't care less |

## • *Facial expressions and gestures* •

Your body language gives out messages about how you are really feeling. Your facial expressions, the way you stand or sit and the **gestures** you use, may not always give the same message as your spoken words!

You are showing negative body language when you do the following:

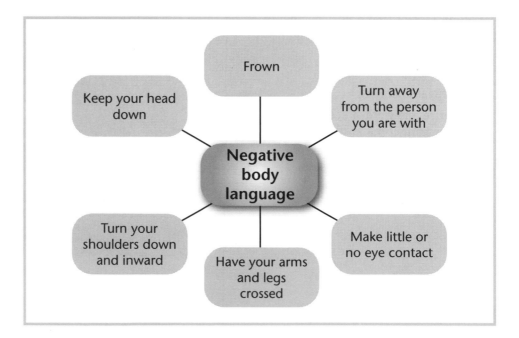

You are showing positive body language when you do the following:

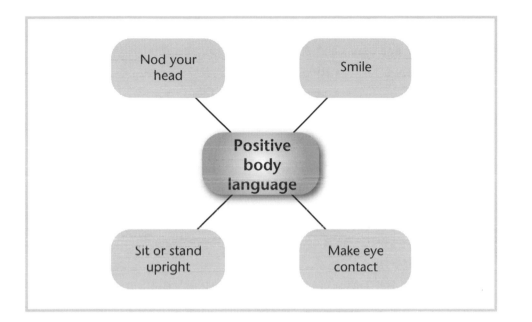

## GIVE IT A GO: identify body language

Look at the cartoon figures below and use the words provided to describe what feelings the people are showing. You may use each word more than once and use more than one word to describe one character.

| | | | |
|---|---|---|---|
| happy | sad | interested | enthusiastic |
| bored | frightened | relaxed | in control |
| angry | superior | professional | nervous |
| unsure | unhappy | uninterested | unfriendly |

## GIVE IT A GO: being positive

Look at the list of negative body language below and, for each point, suggest a positive alternative:

- looking at the floor
- turned away from the customer
- arms crossed in front of body
- sitting slouched over desk
- fingers drumming on table
- blank facial expression.

### • *Welcoming and assisting* •

When entering an organisation, if the staff ignore us we feel unwelcome. If a member of staff looks up, smiles, greets us and asks how to help us, we feel welcome and valued.

### • *Questioning* •

Before you can help your customers you must ask them questions to find out what their needs are. Another good way to build rapport is by asking open questions. These prompt the customer to give us information and not just the answer 'yes' or 'no'.

Open questions always start with one of the following words:

Who?    What?    Why?    When?    Which?    Where?    How?

## GIVE IT A GO: who am I?

Working in small groups, each person should write the name of someone famous and well-known on a post-it note, for example an actor, singer, politician or TV presenter. Stick the note on the forehead of the person on your left. Each person then takes a turn in asking closed questions to guess who they are. The others can only give 'yes' or 'no' as their answer. Count how many questions each person asks before guessing who they are.

In the last activity one open question 'Who am I?' would have provided the answer.

## GIVE IT A GO: open questions

Change the following closed questions to open questions:

- Can I help you?
- Do you want to go in the summer?
- Is it a double room that you would like?
- Is £300 too much to spend?
- Can you come at 2 pm?

## ● *Active listening* ●

In addition to having good questioning skills, you must also show customers that you are paying attention to what they are saying. You do this by active listening, which means that as you listen you respond to what people are saying. You can do this in a variety of ways:

- *nodding*
- *agreeing with the customer*
- *repeating what is said to check your understanding*
- *keeping steady eye contact.*

## ● *Telephone skills* ●

When speaking to a customer on the telephone you must be particularly careful about your tone of voice as that is all customers have to help them make an impression of you. Remember to smile when speaking on the telephone. This lifts your tone of voice and makes you sound more friendly and positive.

When answering the telephone in a customer service role you should:

- *say 'Good morning/afternoon' (don't forget to smile!)*
- *give the name of the organisation*
- *give your name*
- *ask 'How can I help you?'*
- *have a pen and paper ready to write down any details*
- *take a message, if the caller wants to speak to someone who is not available.*

## ● *Recording and relaying messages* ●

If you are asked to take a message for a colleague, it is important that you **relay** all the details to them correctly. Here is a checklist of things you need to cover when you are taking a telephone message:

- *take the caller's name*
- *take the reason for the call*
- *ask who the message is for*
- *take the caller's phone number for returning the call*
- *ask the best time to return the call*
- *repeat the details to ensure your notes are accurate*
- *thank the customer for calling*
- *say goodbye*
- *note the date and time of the call.*

Don't be afraid to ask the customer to spell out words or names that you are unsure of.

**GLOSSARY**

**Relay** means to pass on the accurate message to the correct person.

**WHAT if?**

### ... *you failed to pass on an important message?*

What effect could it have on your team's customer service?

## EVIDENCE ACTIVITY (P4) (P5)

### *Telephone message form*

1 Design a telephone message form to be used when taking messages from customers for colleagues who are not available at that time. Remember to include the following details:

- date and time of call
- who the call was for
- the best time to make the return call
- the customer's name and return telephone number
- details of the customer's message.

2 In pairs, take it in turns to be the customer and the employee answering the telephone. Use the following scenarios:

**a** Miss Sula phones to speak to your manager. She wants to complain about her stay in your hotel. It was not what she expected.

**b** Mr Fouquet gave your colleague, Mohammed, details of a planned visit to the south of France. He wants to know what details Mohammed has found out so far.

Complete the call, ensuring that the employee fills out the message form with all the necessary details. Tape record your conversation to hear how you sounded and discuss what changes to your voice you could make.

**EVIDENCE ACTIVITY** M2

*Providing information positively*

1  Visit your local Tourist Information Centre and collect leaflets about different hotels, visitor attractions and activities.

2  In pairs, do a role play with one person playing an information assistant in a Tourist Information Centre (TIC) and the other a customer. Using leaflets from your local TIC, demonstrate the following:

   • a friendly welcome
   • asking open questions to find out how you can help the customer
   • providing the information required in a helpful and efficient manner.

This will provide evidence towards your communication key skill.

# Care and service

Everyone can provide a certain level of care and service. However, staff who care most and work hard to get the best for their customers will provide the best customer service.

Customer service is directly related to sales and an organisation making a profit. Excellent customer service will encourage customers to buy the product or service and so the organisation will increase sales and profit.

## Care

We can show we care about serving a customer well by:

⊃  *showing attentiveness*
⊃  *having a positive attitude*
⊃  *selecting and providing accurate and appropriate information*
⊃  *exceeding customer expectations.*

### ● *Attentiveness* ●

Attentiveness means paying attention to your customer and not being distracted by other things. An example of attentiveness could be a travel agent who is helping a customer booking a holiday. She ignores her two colleagues, who are having a discussion at the next desk, and instead concentrates on booking the right holiday for her customer.

⌒◯ **THINK ABOUT IT**

How would the customer feel if the person helping them was not concentrating and seemed more interested in other colleagues, who were discussing what they did at the weekend?

## ● *Attitude* ●

'He always sees the glass as half full.' Have you ever heard someone talking about a friend in this way? It is a saying that means that the person being described always sees the positive side of things. You have already discussed Alison, in the case study on page 60, and how she would perhaps enjoy life more if she had a positive attitude. A customer booking a late deal for a bargain price may be unhappy about the night flights. However, a positive travel agent might suggest that at night it will be a quicker journey to the airport as there will be less traffic on the roads, or that the **night flights** reduce the holiday cost, so the customer will have even more money to spend while on holiday!

> **GLOSSARY**
>
> **Night flights** are flights that depart between 11 pm and 6 am.

## ● *Selecting and providing accurate and appropriate information* ●

Good customer service means giving customers information that is correct and useful to them. The list below provides some examples of how to do this:

▱ *An elderly person making a hotel reservation is likely to want a hotel in a quiet area. Therefore you might not give information about hotels near bars and night clubs.*

▱ *A visitor to a tourist information centre may ask for directions to a visitor attraction. It would be useful to also give the opening hours and entry costs.*

▱ *Two young men in their 20s going to Tenerife on holiday may not be interested in tours of the island, but might prefer to have information on the best resort for nightlife.*

## ● *Exceeding customer expectations* ●

This is when a customer asks us for assistance and we automatically give extra help and information.

## ● *Over-promise and under-deliver* ●

If you are unable to help customers immediately, you should be honest and explain why you cannot, advise what you will do and agree when you will contact them to confirm what you have done. The customer will then have **realistic** expectations.

Over-promising is when you offer more than you can deliver.

> **GLOSSARY**
>
> **Realistic** means something we know we can achieve/complete.

## CASE STUDY – I'M IMPRESSED!

Mr and Mrs Goldstein arrived at the Royal Orchid Hotel in Singapore. While they were checking in at reception the barman brought them each a glass of champagne to welcome them. The receptionist asked if they would like to reserve a table in the restaurant that evening and quickly telephoned the head chef to check what vegetarian options there were for Mrs Goldstein. She also asked which newspaper they would like to be delivered to their door the next morning.

The porter arrived at their side to carry their luggage to their room. There was a bowl of fresh fruit and a vase of beautiful fresh flowers in the room to greet them. A few minutes later, one of the housekeeping staff knocked at the door and asked if everything was alright.

They decided to check out the leisure centre in the hotel, where they were met by a smiling assistant who took them around and explained in detail the facilities available, the opening times, and where to collect the white fluffy towels available for guests to use. She answered their questions about the gym equipment and demonstrated how to use them.

Later, when Mr and Mrs Goldstein were having a drink in the comfortable hotel bar (and enjoying the complimentary nibbles) they agreed that the Royal Orchid Hotel was definitely exceeding their expectations!

- Identify and write down the different actions that impressed the hotel guests.
- Discuss what impact each made.
- How difficult do you think it was for each hotel employee to provide this service?

## CASE STUDY – A BUSY DAY

Jack is an enthusiastic trainee with a well-known travel agency. He enjoys his job and always tries to be very helpful with every customer. Today has been a busy Saturday. Here are the details of two of the customers he served today:

1 Mrs Smith booked a holiday to Cyprus, her first visit, and Jack said that he would contact the Cyprus National Tourist Board in London to request they send her information on the country. Unfortunately, Jack started to serve another customer immediately and forgot all about phoning the tourist board.

2 At about 11.30 am Jack answered the telephone. It was Mr Makowski, who wanted to speak to the manager about his round-the-world cruise. Jack promised that the manager would phone Mr Makowski in the next ten minutes. However, the travel agency was still very busy and it was half an hour later before Jack had a chance to give the message to his manager.

- How will Mrs Smith and Mr Makowski feel about the service they have each received?

- What would you suggest Jack should have done, or said, to be able to keep his promises?

Under-delivering is when we say we will do something and then do not do it. For example, when a holiday isn't how it was described and the customer is disappointed.

It is good to want to provide the best service for your customers. However, you must be honest about what you can deliver.

# Service

In this section you will look at different aspects of providing service to your internal and external customers.

### ● *Assisting customers* ●

Some customers need special assistance from staff to meet their needs and help them to enjoy the product being offered. The list below shows some examples of this.

- *An elderly traveller may need to be taken from the airport check-in desk to the departure gate on a motorised buggy.*
- *A businessman hosting a meeting in a hotel may need the hotel staff to help him set up computer equipment in the meeting room.*
- *A member of staff at a tourist attraction may need to escort a guest in a wheelchair through a more convenient entrance than the turnstiles.*

### ● *Offering help* ●

Some people are independent and like to do as much as possible for themselves. However, others are less confident and do appreciate it when someone offers to help. You should offer help sensitively to find out what type of customer you have and whether they would welcome your assistance.

▲ **Learn to offer help sensitively**

## GIVE IT A GO: offering help

Think about the following situations. What could you ask each of the following customers to see if they would like your help? Make your questions as friendly and helpful as you can.

- You work on the reception of a large hotel and see a customer in a wheelchair trying to negotiate the revolving doors at the hotel entrance.
- You work in a tourist information centre and while out during your lunch break, still in uniform, you observe two overseas visitors with confused looks on their faces looking very carefully at a map of your town.
- You work for an airline as air cabin crew and just before one flight is about to take off, you see a passenger trying to get her hand luggage into the overhead locker.

## • *Communicating* •

Some problems happen because people do not talk to each other and keep customers informed about what is happening. For example, when a customer makes a complaint, it may need to be investigated and other organisations contacted to find out what happened and to agree an acceptable solution with the customer. This can take some time. To keep customers satisfied while this is happening, you need to communicate with them. That way they know they have not been forgotten and it reassures them that investigations are still taking place.

WHAT **if?**

### ... *you receive a complaint?*

A customer complains to you about the dirty swimming pool at the hotel. You take a note of all the details and say that you will investigate. How will the customer feel if you have not made contact three weeks later?

## • *Providing products or services* •

Hospitality, travel and tourism organisations spend a great deal of money advertising their products. Some examples include:

- *advertisements on TV*
- *advertisements in newspapers and magazines*
- *posters showing special offers for meals displayed in hotels and restaurants*
- *late holiday deals and discounts advertised in travel agency windows.*

These all help to create customer expectations about the product or service you are providing. As you have seen, if these expectations are not met the chances are customers will not return to your company in future.

More importantly, the description of products is covered by law. Customers have rights!

All organisations must comply with the Trade Descriptions Act 1972. This Act states that any description of a product or service must be truthful at the time that it was written and that if circumstances change, the organisation must inform customers of the changes. Therefore it would be breaking the law to describe a holiday destination as quiet and peaceful in a brochure if the resort was adjacent to the main airport and frequently subject to aircraft noise.

## GLOSSARY

**Point of departure** is the place you depart from when you are taking a journey, such as a bus stop, coach or railway station or airport.

## ● *Delivery times and dates* ●

Trains, planes, buses and coaches all operate to a timetable and all transport companies aim to operate their fleet of vehicles as near to the timetable as possible. Travellers must ensure they have enough time to get to their **point of departure** when making a journey. The 24-hour clock is used for all travel times. This ensures that passengers do not mistake a 6 am flight departure for a 6 pm departure. On the 24-hour clock 6 am is 0600 hrs and 6 pm is 1800 hrs.

## GIVE IT A GO: 24-hour clock

Convert the times given in am and pm below to the 24-hour format. The first example has been completed for you.

| | |
| --- | --- |
| 4.15 pm | 1615 hrs |
| 4.30 am | |
| 11.30 pm | |
| 1 am | |
| 2.15 pm | |
| 7.45 pm | |
| 8 pm | |

▲ Fresh food has to arrive on time

Keeping to dates and schedules is equally important for internal customers. Chefs in restaurants and hotels rely on goods to be delivered on the correct day and time. Many chefs prefer to cook with fresh food, which has to be ordered every day to ensure quality products are cooked and served to customers.

## ● *Responding to changes in customer needs* ●

Jobs which require employees to deal with customers are popular because most of us enjoy the variety and challenges that dealing with people provides. No two days are exactly the same – and no two customers are the same! By asking open questions you can find out customers' needs and offer the best product for them. However, customers can, and do, change their minds, or their circumstances may change. The following case study provides an example.

▲ Family holidays are popular

## CASE STUDY – CHANGES AND UPDATES

Mrs Wilson liked booking her holiday with Penny, her favourite travel consultant in her local travel agent. In January she had booked a one-week holiday to Majorca for her and her husband and their two daughters, aged 13 and 9. They had a family room in the four-star Santa Lucia Hotel in Palma Nova. Two weeks later her husband's parents decided that they would join them and help with looking after the girls, so she requested that a twin room was added. Then the family decided that it would be better to stay for two weeks and the booking was amended. A month later the whole family received invitations to a big family wedding taking place at home during the second week of the holiday, so their departure date had to be brought forward one week. Shortly after, Mrs Wilson decided that it would be better if they left from London Luton Airport, not Gatwick, so she called in to see Penny to make the changes. Reading the brochure one evening, Mrs Wilson realised that they could request sea view rooms, so she telephoned Penny the next day to add this to the booking. Later, when she was paying the balance payment Mrs Wilson asked Penny to contact the tour operator to advise about vegetarian meals for her elder daughter. Two weeks before departure, Mr Wilson broke a bone in his left arm, which had to be in a plaster cast and Mrs Wilson called in to see Penny to arrange for special assistance at both departure and arrival airports.

- Penny always helped Mrs Wilson in a friendly and professional manner. How do you think this made Mrs Wilson feel?
- What might happen if Penny did not respond in a positive way?

### ● *Seeking assistance when required* ●

It is not necessary, nor is it always possible, to know everything about the products and services your organisation offers. Customers do not expect you to know all the information, but they do expect you to know where to find the information or know who to ask. When you first start a new job, there may be many customers' questions that you cannot answer and you will have to ask a colleague for help.

▲ Ask a colleague for help if you cannot answer a customer's question

## GIVE IT A GO: getting help

You have started a new job as a trainee receptionist in a large three-star hotel and are asked many questions by hotel guests. Match each guest's question below with the best member of staff to help you with their request.

| | Guest question | | Best person to ask |
|---|---|---|---|
| 1 | A guest would like vegetarian meals in the hotel restaurant. | A | Bar Manager |
| 2 | A guest would like to know if shower gel and shampoo are provided in the showers in the leisure centre. | B | Housekeeping staff |
| 3 | A couple need a cot in their double room for their baby. | C | Leisure centre staff |
| 4 | Two guests want to know, what time the hotel bar closes in the evenings. | D | Head Porter |
| 5 | An elderly guest wants to arrange a time for her luggage to be collected from her room at the end of her stay. | E | Head Chef |

## • *Organisational limitations and guidelines* •

As an employee, you represent the organisation that employs you. The organisation will have rules and guidelines for you to follow as you do your job. These will help you in many ways. Guidelines might include:

- *the procedure to follow when a customer complains*
- *security procedures – e.g. opening and closing, and getting valuables from the safe*
- *storage of products – e.g. how long fresh foods can be stored in the fridge, keeping flight tickets in a secure safe*
- *dress codes – e.g. uniforms and what clothing to wear and how to look after it.*

## • *Keeping records and information* •

Providing good customer service includes writing information down to help you and your colleagues to continue to provide the best customer service. All hospitality, travel and tourism organisations keep records and information on their customers.

- *A travel agency keeps details of their customers' holiday reservations.*
- *A hotel has records of guests who have stayed and any special **requirements** they have.*

▲ **Keeping records is important**

## GLOSSARY

**Requirements** are what a customer needs.

- Most organisations keep a record of customer complaints and what was done to resolve each situation.
- All organisations have Accident Record Books, which are updated with any accidents that happen on the premises.

## EVIDENCE ACTIVITY

### Holiday recommendation

You have been asked to recommend a holiday for Mrs and Mrs Williams, who are regular customers of the travel agency where you work. You access your computer system and print off a record of their last four holidays booked at your agency. This includes comments that the customers made each time they received a courtesy call from your agency after each holiday.

| Departure date and duration | Destination | Accommodation | Total Cost | Customer comments |
|---|---|---|---|---|
| 10 May 05 07 nights | Cala D'or Majorca | 3-star apartment, self-catering | £600.00 | Liked travelling around the island, didn't like this resort – too many young families. |
| 05 Sep 04 14 nights | Paphos Cyprus | 4-star hotel, B&B | £1250.00 | Liked B&B – able to eat out at lots of the really good local restaurants, lots to do and see around the island. |
| 20 Jan 04 07 nights | Sauze d'Oulx Italy | 3-star hotel, breakfast and evening meal | £1400.00 | Food good in hotel, enjoyed skiing and the other activities available in the resort |
| 07 Aug 03 07 nights | Vilamoura Portugal | 4 star hotel, B&B | £800.00 | Enjoyed the range of excursions, would have liked the hotel to be nearer the centre of the resort (3 miles outside) |

1 In pairs, discuss what the records tell you about Mr and Mrs Williams.

2 Research a hotel and resort for them for a two-week holiday in Turkey in September. Use a selection of 'summer sun' brochures. (These are brochures featuring holidays to sunny destinations, between May and October.)

3 List the reasons why you are recommending this holiday.

# EVIDENCE ACTIVITY

## *Consistently good service*

1 Describe how you can provide consistent customer care and service.

2 Explain why it is important to provide good customer service.

Now we have discussed the importance of communication skills and the care and service we provide customers, it is your turn to demonstrate your own skills in the next activity

# EVIDENCE ACTIVITY

## *Providing excellent service*

Using the information from the sections on communication skills and care and service, work in pairs to demonstrate, through role play, how you would help each of the customers in the scenarios below. Any additional information required can be made up by your customer.

1 Mrs Blackwell is looking for a family holiday (two adults and two children, aged seven and five years) in Ibiza, departing from Manchester in August for two weeks. She would like a three-star hotel with children's clubs in a quiet resort.

2 Yasmin and three friends, all aged 19–20 years, want an apartment holiday in Ayia Napa, Cyprus for two weeks in July. They will fly from Glasgow or Edinburgh airports. They want to be in the centre of all the nightlife!

3 Mr and Mrs Patel would like to stay in a picturesque resort in the Portuguese Algarve. They would like a four-star hotel, bed and breakfast only, flying from Gatwick for one week in May.

4 Navin and Raj are looking for a two-week holiday in Turkey, flying from London Luton airport in June. They would like either an apartment or a three-star hotel. However, it must be a resort where there are watersports available.

**WORK SEARCH**

Check your understanding of the information in this unit by answering the following questions. To help you, the answers can be found in the word search.

1 The name given to the type of customer who helps you do your job. (8)

2 The word to describe what a customer thinks you will do for them. (12)

3 When a customer first meets you, you want to give the right ............. (10)

4 Good ............. is vital to providing good customer service. (13)

5 Many organisations provide a ............. for all staff to wear so that they are easily recognised by customers. (7)

6 When a group of people work well together and help each other do their job. (8)

7 What kind of attitude is best in customer service? (8)

8 Another term for non-verbal communication. (4, 8)

9 When speaking on the telephone, we ............. to lift the tone of our voice. (5)

10 What kind of information should we always give the customer? (8)

| C | L | E | A | Z | O | W | H | M | J | S | D | Z | K | B |
|---|---|---|---|---|---|---|---|---|---|---|---|---|---|---|
| B | H | T | E | L | A | K | M | K | C | E | S | C | R | O |
| B | V | Q | H | X | W | F | G | N | V | F | M | V | O | D |
| W | G | J | G | L | P | G | M | I | X | V | Z | T | W | Y |
| V | X | L | Q | U | X | E | T | V | R | A | L | H | M | L |
| C | O | M | M | U | N | I | C | A | T | I | O | N | A | A |
| H | S | F | Z | P | S | I | Z | T | M | G | M | J | E | N |
| Q | I | H | B | O | Z | Q | F | P | A | U | O | H | T | G |
| H | G | C | P | L | V | C | R | O | Q | T | U | C | H | U |
| S | Y | J | H | M | T | E | E | H | R | J | I | I | W | A |
| M | F | T | A | K | S | H | G | P | E | M | Y | O | U | G |
| I | O | N | K | S | L | A | N | R | E | T | N | I | N | E |
| L | G | I | I | A | C | C | U | R | A | T | E | J | U | S |
| E | N | O | F | S | X | B | J | I | F | W | Z | O | N | B |
| C | N | J | U | M | L | R | Z | T | N | A | K | J | C | G |

# unit 4

## Personal effectiveness

This unit will help you to explore your own potential by carrying out an **audit** of your skills related to the jobs market of the hospitality, travel and tourism sector. You will also draw up a curriculum vitae to present to employers.

*In this unit you will learn about:*

- ▷ how to carry out a personal audit to help find suitable jobs
- ▷ how to explore your potential in relation to suitable jobs
- ▷ how to prepare a personal statement and portfolio to prepare for employment.

## Personal audit

### Vocational skills and interests

When applying for a job, you may be asked to provide information about the work experience you already have. It may be obvious to include information about part-time jobs and work experience that you have had. However, you may have also achieved skills through other activities such as baby-sitting or voluntary work at a community or church organisation, such as an after-school club, the Brownies or the Cubs. Perhaps you have completed some qualifications, such as a Duke of Edinburgh's Award or a first-aid certificate.

## EVIDENCE ACTIVITY  P1

### Audit your job-related skills

Create a table similar to the one below. List all the activities you participate in now and have participated in in the past. List what you do for the activity and then what skills you have learnt by participating in it.

| Activity | My responsibilities, what I did | Skills I learnt by doing this |
| --- | --- | --- |
|  |  |  |

You can also learn a lot about someone from their interests and hobbies. You may have gained other skills and experience from doing these activities too.

## EVIDENCE ACTIVITY  P1

### Identify your job-related skills

Now list your interests and hobbies – what you enjoy doing in your free time. What do you enjoy about them? Create and fill in a table similar to the one below.

| Interest/hobby | Why I like doing this |
| --- | --- |
|  |  |

### GLOSSARY

**Transferable** means that the same skill can be used in a different situation. A **curriculum vitae** is a written summary of your education, qualifications and work experience.

You now have a list of your skills and experiences in these tables. Many of these skills are **transferable**. Future employers will recognise these skills and be more interested in employing you. You will return to this information to complete your **curriculum vitae**.

# Personal skills and behaviour

Employers and customers expect employees to behave in a professional manner. This includes:

- *your spoken language (verbal)*
- *your behaviour*
- *your appearance*
- *your body language (non-verbal).*

In Unit 3 you discussed these and how they are connected to customer service. In this unit you will think about how these relate to you personally.

## ● *Behaviour* ●

As you saw in the Unit 3, how you behave at work contributes to the overall impression you give your customers and colleagues. It can affect your standard of work.

### CASE STUDY – ACCEPTABLE BEHAVIOUR?

Jon, Navin, Will and Ahsel are great friends. They went to secondary school together and kept in touch when they left school. Ahsel went to college, Navin to university, Jon completed an apprenticeship and Will started work. They enjoy their weekends and have a wild time, clubbing until about 4 am, then sleeping until after midday. They all have tattoos on their arms. They all have shaved heads apart from Navin, who has a more conventional short hair cut. Will and Ahsel each wear an earring in their right ear. The boys swear most of the time and all have loud voices – not the sort of people you would want to meet in a quiet street late at night! This is how they behave in their own time, but this would be unacceptable behaviour at work.

However, it is very different at work, where they each have a responsible job. Jon is the manager of a large travel agency; Navin is a human resources manager for a large chain of restaurants; Will is an airline reservations duty manager and Ahsel teaches hospitality at the local college of further education. They all know that at work they must **modify** their behaviour and act in a responsible and mature way. They all dress smartly. Jon and Will wear their company uniforms and none of them swears at work. Their colleagues would describe them as mature and sensible adults.

#### GLOSSARY

**Modify** means to change slightly.

Discuss the following questions with the whole class:

- How responsible do the boys sound when you have read about their behaviour in their free time?
- How surprised were you to learn what jobs they have?
- What are the main differences in their behaviour in their free time and at work?
- How would the behaviour they portray at weekends be viewed at work?

# Personal skills

▲ **Your individual style will need to be modified in the workplace**

## ● *Appearance* ●

You already know that your appearance is an important factor in employment. In your free time you probably choose to dress in casual clothes. All of us sometimes look a bit scruffy when we are in a hurry or are feeling relaxed at home! An employer will require you to present yourself in a particular way and this might mean wearing a uniform or formal dress. There are two main reasons for this:

▷ *safety* – *some jobs require employees to wear certain clothes for safety reasons*
▷ *standards* – *some jobs require employees to wear a uniform or formal clothes in order to be ambassadors for their company.*

### THINK ABOUT IT

Whatever style of clothes you prefer personally, you need to be aware of what image it gives to others. What do you think your appearance might tell an interviewer about you?

## ● *Body language and posture* ●

In Unit 3 you saw how your body language can confirm what you are saying or give away your true feelings. While body language is **subconscious**, we can teach ourselves to be more aware of our own and other people's body language, to see if it matches what the other person is actually saying!

## Inter-personal skills

The hospitality, travel and tourism sector is known as a 'people business': one where you will be dealing with people face to face most of the time. You may also be working as part of a team, so how well you are able to work with other people is as important as the skills, experience and knowledge you have.

**GLOSSARY**

**Subconscious** means existing without you being aware of it.

## GIVE IT A GO: relating to colleagues

1 What work teams can you think of in the hospitality, travel and tourism sector? You have already looked at some in earlier units, such as bar staff and travel agency sales consultants.

2 What are the benefits of each team member getting on with the others in the team?

# Your potential

## Assessment of strengths and weaknesses

Now that you have a list of your skills and the activities you enjoy, you can start to identify what your 'strengths' and 'weaknesses' are. This is called a self-assessment and involves looking honestly at how well we do things and deciding whether we have the skills to do a job that appeals to us. Assessment by others is, for example, when an employer interviews someone for a job.

## EVIDENCE ACTIVITY  P3

*Your strengths and weaknesses*

1 Read the skills and qualities in the table below and discuss the following in your group:

• What does each one mean?

• How important are these skills at work?

Create a copy of the table below and decide whether each skill or quality is a strength or a weakness. Then place a ✓ in the third column if you think this is a strength for you or a ✗ if it is a weakness.

| Skill / action | Strength or weakness | Me? |
|---|---|---|
| Able to work independently | | |
| Able to work with others | | |
| Impatient | | |
| Punctual | | |
| Quiet and shy | | |
| Disorganised | | |
| Able to give clear instructions | | |
| Able to follow instructions | | |

| Skill / action | Strength or weakness | Me? |
|---|---|---|
| Good timekeeping | | |
| Always swearing | | |
| Talking fast | | |
| Reliable | | |
| Always gossiping | | |
| Smart appearance | | |
| Unreliable | | |
| Always late | | |
| Enthusiastic | | |
| Honest | | |
| Hard working | | |
| Forgetful | | |
| Illegible handwriting | | |
| Numerate | | |
| Always talking | | |
| Makes no eye contact | | |
| Able to listen | | |
| Confident | | |
| Does not listen | | |
| Scowls all the time | | |
| Uses initiative | | |
| Desires to learn new skills | | |
| **Good administrative ability** | | |
| **Good customer focus** | | |

## GLOSSARY

Someone who has **good administrative ability** is organised and completes paperwork neatly and accurately.

## GLOSSARY

An employee with **good customer focus** is someone who always puts themselves in the customer's position and works hard to meet their customers' needs.

2  It is a good idea to check your self-assessment with others. You may find that you have been hard on yourself about some things. Assessment by others can help you to understand what areas you need to develop.

## Matching strengths to job roles

The jobs that you will be best at and enjoy the most will be those where the job descriptions and personal specifications most match your strengths. A job description gives details of the tasks and responsibilities of a job. Many employers give their staff job descriptions, as you saw in Unit 2. A personal specification describes the personal skills that are needed to do a job effectively. Employers often use these to decide if they will interview someone for a job. They look at a person's job application and if they have many of the skills they will interview you for the job.

### CASE STUDY – SO YOU WOULD LIKE TO BE A RESORT REPRESENTATIVE?

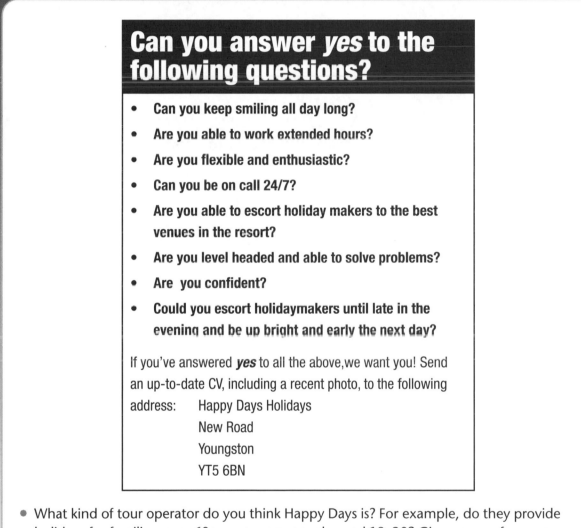

# Can you answer *yes* to the following questions?

- Can you keep smiling all day long?
- Are you able to work extended hours?
- Are you flexible and enthusiastic?
- Can you be on call 24/7?
- Are you able to escort holiday makers to the best venues in the resort?
- Are you level headed and able to solve problems?
- Are you confident?
- Could you escort holidaymakers until late in the evening and be up bright and early the next day?

If you've answered *yes* to all the above, we want you! Send an up-to-date CV, including a recent photo, to the following address:    Happy Days Holidays
New Road
Youngston
YT5 6BN

- What kind of tour operator do you think Happy Days is? For example, do they provide holidays for families, over 60s or younger people aged 18–30? Give reasons for your answer.

What jobs interest you? There are various sources of information that you can use to find out about available jobs, such as:

- *websites of hospitality, travel and tourism organisations on the Internet*
- *recruitment websites on the Internet*
- *national and local newspapers*

- *hospitality, travel and tourism trade journals and newspapers*
- *careers services*
- *your school or college will have a department that provides information on most types of jobs and vacancies in your local area*
- *your local job centre displays information on vacancies and the staff can also give advice on job opportunities and training schemes in your area.*
- *employment agencies that help many employers fill staff vacancies.*

Using these sources of information will help you make the right decisions about which jobs you are well matched to do and could apply for.

## EVIDENCE ACTIVITY · P2

### Match your skills to jobs in hospitality, travel and tourism

Use the sources of information listed above to find out about the jobs that interest you.

- Keep a copy of the details of a range of jobs that you think you might consider in future.
- To help find the jobs that you are most suited to, highlight the descriptions that match your strengths.
- Make a list of the skills that you would like to improve and any new ones you would like to develop.

## Action plan

Having identified your strengths and weaknesses you can now plan what to do to improve your skills and experience. One way of doing this is to write an action plan. Personal development would include things like improving your body language and posture, whereas work-based development could include computer or product training. Action plans can be used for both.

An action plan will set out the steps you need to take to achieve your goals and fulfil your potential. It details the following:

- *the goal or target – what you want to do*
- *the timescale – when you would like to do it*
- *who you might need to help you*
- *what resources you need to complete the task*
- *monitoring and reviews.*

### ● *Monitoring and review* ●

Monitoring is an important task in any action plan. It is when you check your progress in order to keep on track with your targets. Having some short-term targets can help you feel a sense of satisfaction. As you complete them, you know that you are moving towards your goal. Monitoring also allows you to review your plan. Maybe some targets are too ambitious? Perhaps you can achieve more? It is an opportunity to change your action plan to fit your goals.

## ● *Evaluation* ●

Evaluation means taking time to think about your achievements. It helps you understand how well you feel you achieved your goals and what further action is required. You can evaluate at the end of your action plan or you can evaluate each target.

Some questions you could ask yourself are:

▭ *How many tasks have I completed in full?*
▭ *Which tasks have I started, but not completed?*
▭ *Which tasks do I like least?*
▭ *Which tasks have helped me the most?*

## EVIDENCE ACTIVITY  P4

### *Prepare your action plan*

Write an action plan in which you:

- name your goal – e.g. this might be the job you would like to be doing in three years' time
- match your skills and qualities to the job and identify skills targets
- identify short-term targets
- identify long-term targets
- identify any qualifications you will need to achieve
- set up a timetable with:
  – dates for achieving each target
  – dates for checking progress and reviewing your plan
- list what resources you will need
- list people who might be able to help you achieve your goal.

# Personal statement and portfolio

There are three types of paperwork used when applying for jobs:

- *letters of application*
- *your curriculum vitae*
- *application forms.*

In Unit 3 you looked at the importance of first impressions. Everything you learned about meeting people or entering an organisation holds true when you are applying for a job. However, your written correspondence will also give the reader a first impression of you. Therefore you must ensure that your spelling and grammar are correct as well as including relevant information about yourself.

## Letter of application

You send a letter of application when you are introducing yourself to an organisation because you want to apply for a job. You may be writing concerning a job, which has been advertised, or making a general enquiry about vacancies. If you have seen a job advertised, the organisation may then send you an application form. If you are making a general enquiry, you do not have any formal forms to complete.

Opposite is an example of a letter of application. The key below explains the different features to note in the letter.

1 Include your address and the date.

2 Write to a specific person (if you can) and ensure the address is correct.

3 Say what job you are applying for.

4 Say where you saw the job advertised.

5 Give your age.

6 List your most recent relevant qualifications.

7 Say why you want the job.

8 Say what relevant skills and experience you have.

9 Include brief details about yourself and your interests.

10 Include the details of two referees.

11 End the letter correctly: 'yours sincerely' if you know the name of the person, or if you are writing to 'Dear Sir/Madam, 'yours faithfully'.

(1) 17 Meadow Road
Middletown
MD10 8WN

15 June 2005

Mr Wright
Personnel Manager (2)
Value Travel
36 High Street
Middletown
MD1 9YT

Dear Mr Wright

RE: Trainee Travel Sales Consultant post (3)

I would like to enquire about the vacancy you advertised in the Middletown Times on 12 June 2005 for a trainee travel sales consultant. (4)

(5) I am 17 years of age and left Middletown College in June this year after successfully completing my BTEC Introductory Certificate in Hospitality, Travel and Tourism. I achieved an overall grade of Merit. During the one-year full-time course, I studied a range of travel and tourism subjects, including customer service, marketing and planning itineraries, as well as Skills for Life in information technology, communication and numeracy. (6)

I would really like to work for Value Travel because it has a good reputation and is a busy and successful travel agency. I am interested in the training and experience you offer and the opportunities within the company for career progression. (7)

While at college I worked part-time in a large high street clothes retailer and I have been working full-time as a waitress in a local golf club since finishing my course. (8)

(9) I enjoy keeping fit and belong to my local gym, where I regularly attend exercise classes. I like to socialise with my friends, go to the cinema and play in a ladies football team every Sunday. I am a friendly, outgoing person and enjoy meeting people and the challenge of being busy and doing something different every day. If you wish to obtain references, please contact:

Miss K Bates                                  Mrs G Short                          (10)
Lecturer – Travel and Tourism       Manager
Middletown College                        Fashion Wise
Cornfield Way                                 135 High Street
Middletown                                     Middletown
MD5 4DL                                         MD1 7UL

I am available to come for an interview at any time.

Yours sincerely (11)

Farzana Shah

As with any business letter, a professional image is created by word-processing your letter. Make sure your envelope is the same colour as your paper. White or cream is best. Use a first-class stamp. Always ask your **referee's** permission before sending in their details.

**GLOSSARY**

A **referee** is someone who is willing to give an interviewer an opinion on your character when you are applying for a job.

## GIVE IT A GO: impress me please!

**1** Read the following letter.

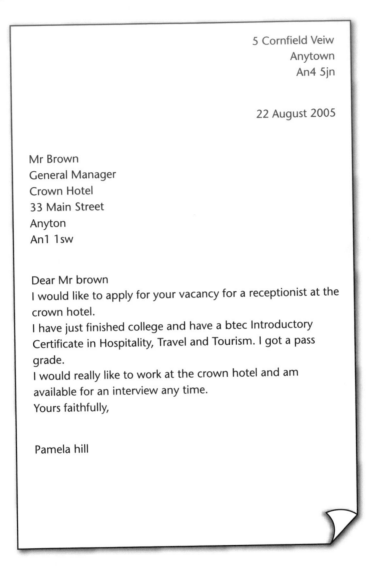

5 Cornfield Veiw
Anytown
An4 5jn

22 August 2005

Mr Brown
General Manager
Crown Hotel
33 Main Street
Anyton
An1 1sw

Dear Mr brown
I would like to apply for your vacancy for a receptionist at the
crown hotel.
I have just finished college and have a btec Introductory
Certificate in Hospitality, Travel and Tourism. I got a pass
grade.
I would really like to work at the crown hotel and am
available for an interview any time.
Yours faithfully,

Pamela hill

- Identify the spelling and grammar mistakes in the letter above.
- Do you think Pamela has impressed this employer?
- What additional information could Pamela have included?
- Rewrite the letter for Pamela. Make up any additional information you feel would make Mr Brown more interested in meeting her.

**2** Now choose one of the jobs you found for the evidence activity on page 88. Write your own letter of application. Word-process your letter. Ask your tutor to check your letter.

# Your CV

Your CV – curriculum vitae (record of life) – is a formal document that gives an employer valuable information about you and will help them decide whether they should interview you for their vacancy. Your CV should be no longer than two pages of A4, and preferably only one. It should include the following information about you:

- **Name and address** – *include your contact telephone numbers and email address.*
- **Personal details** – *date of birth, and some people like to include a passport photo.*
- **Personal statement** – *a short paragraph in which you describe yourself, your personality and attitude to work. This adds some personal details to the qualification information you have included in your CV.*
- **Education details** – *which secondary schools and colleges you attended, the dates and grades of the qualifications you achieved.*
- **Employment details** – *dates of employment, name of organisation, position held and responsibilities. Include part-time work and work experience, if relevant.*
- **Interests and hobbies** – *list any hobbies or interests that show your skills and qualities.*
- **Other information** – *this could include whether you hold a full driving licence, first-aid certificate or, for a travel job, where you have travelled.*
- **Referees** – *Usually you are required to provide the names and addresses of two willing referees. The employer may wish to ask them for a reference before taking you on. They should either be from school, college or somewhere you have worked. If this is not possible, then professionals who have known you for at least two years would be suitable.*

Remember to:

- *make your CV relevant to the job that you are applying for*
- *be truthful*
- *be accurate*
- *use an easy-to-read font and layout*
- *use good-quality white or cream paper to give a professional look.*

An example of a CV is shown on page 94.

## Curriculum Vitae

| Name: | Janet Collins |
| --- | --- |
| Address: | 51 Meadow View<br>Highbury<br>HG8 6RY |
| Telephone: | 01234 567890 |
| Date of Birth: | 15 June 1988 |
| Personal Statement: | I am a friendly and outgoing person. I enjoy meeting people and like jobs where I work with colleagues in a team. I use my initiative and like to work towards targets that have been set for me. I am hard-working and enjoy receiving training and trying something new. |

### Education:

| Dates | School/college | Qualification | |
| --- | --- | --- | --- |
| Sept 2004 – June 2005 | Highbury College of FE | BTEC Introductory Certificate in Hospitality, Travel and Tourism<br>MERIT | |
| Sept 1999–June 2004 | Meadow Secondary School Highbury | GCSE English<br>Maths<br>Science<br>History<br>Business | D<br>E<br>DD<br>E<br>EE |

### Employment:

| Dates | Company | Role |
| --- | --- | --- |
| Aug 2004 – to date | Fashion House | Team Member – receiving deliveries, displaying merchandise and serving customers |
| June 2003 – July 2004 | Millers' News | Shop Assistant – sorting newspapers for delivery, serving customers, stacking shelves |

| Interests: | I belong to a local drama group and a dance school. I have won National Certificates for dance at County and National levels. I babysit regularly and enjoy shopping and listening to music with my friends. |
| --- | --- |
| Additional information: | I have a Duke of Edinburgh Bronze Award. |
| Referees: | Mr I Roberts<br>Lecturer – Travel and Tourism<br>Highbury College of FE<br>Highbury<br>HG1 2BN | Mrs C Brown<br>Manager<br>Fashion House<br>Highbury<br>HG1 1AS |

▲ An example of a curriculum vitae

# EVIDENCE ACTIVITY  P5

## Writing a CV

Now write your own CV using a computer. Take care to lay out the information clearly and check your spelling and grammar. Ask your tutor to check your work.

## • Completing an application form •

Some organisations have application forms and ask all applicants to complete one when applying for a job. It helps the employer to have the same information about every applicant so they can compare them more easily. Sometimes your CV is not needed if there is an application form.

Before completing an application form, read all the instructions carefully. You usually have to use a black ball-point pen (as this photocopies better than other colours). Sometimes you are asked to write in capital letters. A good tip is to photocopy the form and practise by completing the photocopy first. When you are happy with the information you wish to use, you can complete the original form neatly and accurately.

## GIVE IT A GO: practice makes perfect

Obtain an application form from two organisations you would like to work for. Photocopy the forms and complete the copies. Ask your tutor to check your completed forms.

### ● *Preparing for interview* ●

When the employer has received your letter of application and accompanying CV or application form, a member of staff may telephone you to arrange an interview time. How you sound and what you say will add to the impression that the employer already has of you from your application.

As you saw in Unit 3, because you cannot see who you are speaking to on the telephone, how your voice sounds is even more important. The key things to remember are:

▷ *smile – the tone of your voice will lift and you will sound friendlier*
▷ *be aware of the words you are using. Try not to repeat yourself or say the same word again and again*
▷ *be polite and speak clearly.*

## GIVE IT A GO: telephone skills

In pairs, one person should play the role of the employer and the other the job applicant. You are arranging a date and time for your interview by telephone. Tape record your telephone conversation.
• How did you sound?
• What words did you use?
• What improvements or changes would you make?
Repeat this activity several times, changing roles, until you are satisfied with your performance.

You have been invited to an interview! You have received a letter from the organisation, confirming your interview details. To continue to give the best impression you must plan for the interview. If you are well prepared you will feel more confident. Make sure that you:

▷ *arrive at least 15 minutes before your interview time*
▷ *check the transport times in advance and decide what time you must leave home*
▷ *decide what you will wear in advance*

▲ **Make sure you are ready for your interview**

> ▭ *the day before the interview check that your clothes are clean and ironed and lay them out ready*
> ▭ *put the paperwork that you are taking with you into a neat folder (e.g. CV, school and college certificates and copies of personal references)*
> ▭ *find out as much about the organisation and job as possible*
> ▭ *prepare a list of questions that you would like to ask the interviewer (you may cover most of them during the interview), however, it is very impressive to have at least one question when the interviewer asks, 'What questions do you have?'*

## WHAT if?

### ... you have been invited to an interview?

What clothes are best to wear at an interview to help you give the best impression of yourself?

## GIVE IT A GO: I have a question ...

Make a list of questions you could ask a future employer. You may want to look back to Unit 2 where you investigated terms and conditions. What areas would you want to ask about? Include subjects such as training, career opportunities and dress code.

Word-process the list so it looks professional and you can take it with you to future interviews to use as an **aide-memoire**.

### GLOSSARY

An **aide-memoire** is something that you have written down to help you remember.

## GIVE IT A GO: the interview

In groups of three, take the role of the applicant, the interviewer and an observer. You are going to take part in a role play of an interview for one of your chosen jobs. The interviewer and the applicant should prepare written questions in advance. The observer should make observation notes and give feedback to the applicant about:

- their dress
- behaviour
- answers to questions
- preparation.

Each person should take their turn at all three roles.

▲ **An interview is a two-way process**

# Portfolio

Your portfolio is the folder which contains evidence of the work that you have completed towards your qualification. Your completed portfolio can be taken with you to interviews to show the person interviewing you the skills that you have achieved.

## EVIDENCE ACTIVITY (P1) (P2) (P3) (P4) (P5)

### Collecting your evidence

Choose a suitable folder that you are going to use to present your completed portfolio.

You might like to consider buying A4-sized plastic wallets to keep your documents in good condition inside the portfolio.

Put the following documents from this unit inside your portfolio:

- curriculum vitae
- completed application forms
- letters of application
- replies received from employers
- observation reports of role plays you participated in
- your list of questions for a future employer.

```
A C G W J M
B E Z O K V
S E A R C H
R F I D L O
```

Check your understanding of the information in this unit by answering the following questions. Then find the answers in the wordsearch.

1  Something that you are good at is called a ................. (8)

2  Employers and customers expect employees to behave in a ................. manner. (12)

3  An alternative name for someone who represents a company, organisation or country. (10)

4  Your record of qualifications and work experience. (10, 5)

5  You write a letter of ................. when you are introducing yourself to an organisation because you want to apply for a job. (11)

6  If you know the name of the person you are writing to, you end your letter with 'Yours .................' (9)

7  This details the tasks and responsibilities of a job. (3, 11)

8  The meeting you attend to, hopefully, get a new job. (9)

9  The colour of ink you should usually complete official forms in. (5)

10  The name given to the folder containing the examples of work you have completed for your qualification. (9)

```
F N S Q Z E Q Z W U A I N M G
X Y O A T J Y E Y Y Y O H T K
E A T I V M U L U C I R R U C
H L S W T N K V D T N O P L A
K T F I L P E H A W T N T A L
E N G Y N V I C F Y E D Y N B
F C O N I C I R D I R A O O U
Q U Q S E L E N C F V G O I P
R E G C P R L R G S I V F S G
E G Q P E G T Y E B E S P S F
Q D A A Y S H S T L W D V E K
A M B A S S A D O R Y R B F O
O I L O F T R O P Q H E L O Y
T U A C Y P S C S Y W I G R J
C G W E B O P X I T I E K P W
```

# unit 5

## Social responsibility at work

This unit looks at the contribution that all employees can make to the people and the organisation that they work for. In this unit you will study the working environment and why it is important to have legislation to protect people while they are at work. You will also look at and consider the wider influence that you might have on society through the environmental issues that arise at work.

*In this unit you will learn about:*

⬭ environmental issues at work
⬭ how the law affects people at work.

## Environmental issues at work

### Energy conservation and recycling

In the year 2002/03, the government recorded 25.8 million tonnes of household waste in England, which represented 24 kg per household. Many of us have now become used to having more than one dustbin at home for our rubbish. Some local councils in the United Kingdom now provide households with different colour-coded bins for different items – for general waste, paper, tin cans and garden waste. It is no different in the hospitality and travel and tourism sector. All businesses produce waste.

## GIVE IT A GO: the colour of your bins

What colour bins are used in your local authority? Why do we now have different types of dustbins? Does this make the collection of household waste very expensive?

▲ **What a lot of waste!**

It is a simple fact of our world that we produce waste and that this waste has to be disposed of. Getting rid of waste products costs money. As we are learning, if it is not done carefully, it can damage the planet and the environment in which we live.

### • *Disposal* •

Most of the waste you produce is taken by your local council and buried in the ground at the local waste tip. Environmentalists believe there are many negative results from this method of disposal of waste. For example, it produces dangerous substances that can poison the environment.

## CASE STUDY – MCDONALD'S ENVIRONMENT POLICY

### Environment policies and initiatives

McDonald's recognises it has a responsibility to protect and preserve the environment for future generations and continues to work in partnership with suppliers who work towards **minimisation** of waste and efficient use of energy.

### Litter patrols

As part of their community and environmental policy, McDonald's was the first restaurant in Ireland to introduce and operate 'Litter Patrols' in all restaurants around the country.

### GLOSSARY

**Minimisation** means reducing something to the lowest possible amount. **Streamlining** means to make something more efficient.

### Packaging

All their packaging carries the Tidy Man symbol and has an average recycled content of 71 per cent.

### Other initiatives

From recycling oils to reducing electricity consumption and **streamlining** delivery they leave no stone unturned in their efforts towards conservation.

### The rainforests

McDonald's does not purchase beef which threatens tropical rainforests anywhere in the world.

Source:
http://www.mcdonalds.ie/envir/policy.htm

- Why do you think it is important for McDonald's to have environmentally friendly policies?
- What does it mean when McDonald's describes its packaging as having 'an average recycled content of 71 per cent'?
- What else does McDonald's recycle?

## ⬭ THINK ABOUT IT

What a waste!
Imagine that you are working as a room service attendant. What sort of waste would be produced by doing your job? Think about all of the materials and equipment that you might need to carry out your job effectively. Think about the materials guests might leave behind in their rooms.

## ● *Biodegradable materials* ●

Some rubbish is biodegradable and breaks down in the soil over a period of time. Biodegradable materials are made from natural, biological materials. When these materials are in the ground, **micro-organisms** break them down. A lot of rubbish is not biodegradable and it stays in the ground unchanged for years.

## ● *Conserving resources* ●

It is now recognised that our modern society is using up the earth's natural resources at a rate that is not **sustainable** for the future. An important issue connected to waste disposal is the need to conserve resources.

## ● *Recycling* ●

Recycling converts waste into reusable material. Just like your home, businesses produce a lot of waste that can be recycled.

In the UK 2 million printer cartridges and 15 million mobile phones are thrown away each year! Ink cartridges are one of the easiest things to recycle, yet very few people do. Mobile phones can be recycled too.

> **GLOSSARY**
>
> **Micro-organisms** are small life forms such as bacteria, fungi and viruses.

> **GLOSSARY**
>
> **Sustainable** means that it can be kept going at the same rate over a long period of time, without causing problems to the environment.

## GIVE IT A GO: recycling schemes

Using the Internet try to find some different schemes, organisations and companies that are trying to promote recycling. You will find several and some that particularly relate to hospitality, travel and tourism.

## ● *Energy conservation* ●

Another important part of conserving resources is energy **conservation**. Companies are very concerned with the amount of fuel and energy they use. All organisations use large amounts of energy in their day-to-day business. In hospitality, gas and electricity are used to operate the ovens in the kitchens. Lights and air-conditioning are used

> **GLOSSARY**
>
> **Conservation** means the careful use of resources.

throughout hotels. In travel and tourism similar fuels are used for similar operations but, of course, there are also specialist areas such as aviation fuel for aeroplanes. Cutting down on energy use makes good commercial sense because of the savings organisations can make.

**Energy fact:** Cole & Weber, an office with 30 workers, turns their computers off at night and on weekends. This saves £1500 in energy costs a year – enough to pay for a new computer.

## GIVE IT A GO: how careful are you with energy?

When you are away from home – at school, college or a friend's house – do you 'forget' to conserve energy?

Answer the following questions with a simple yes or no. Be honest!

When you are away from home, do you:

- turn on more lights than you need
- leave lights on when leaving the room for a long period of time
- light the whole room when you only need lighting in one small area
- leave the water running while you wash your hands or brush your teeth
- take longer, hotter, or more frequent baths or showers
- use hot water when it is not necessary
- forget to close doors or windows
- forget to close curtains to keep heat inside
- set the **thermostat** higher or lower than the suggested settings
- leave machinery, such as a computer, on all day – even when it is not being used
- use a machine on and off all day when the task could have been accomplished in one short period of time
- keep the TV or radio on even when not watching or listening
- become an all-around energy waster because 'I am not paying for it'
- allow other people to waste energy without making suggestions on how they could be more conservative
- forget that wasting energy affects you, your family, and the planet?

**Scoring**

Count one point for every 'yes' answer. If your score is:

1 to 3: Thank you! You are energy conscious wherever you go.

4 to 6: Watch out! Do not waste energy just because you are away from home.

Above 6: Shape up! You are wasting money and energy that could be used more efficiently by everyone. Don't save just for you – save for the planet.

### GLOSSARY

**Thermostat** is the device that allows you to control the temperate on a heating system.

An easy way to save energy is to cut down on unnecessary lighting. You can:

- *turn off all lights not in use*
- *use bulbs of lower wattage*
- *use natural sunlight when possible*
- *keep bulbs and fixtures clean*
- *focus light on your task*
- *use fluorescent lights wherever possible.*

▲ **Cut down on lighting!**

## GIVE IT A GO: cutting down energy waste

If you have a part-time job at the moment, think about how you might cut down on energy waste in your workplace. Share your ideas with your supervisor and fellow workers.

### • *Attitudes* •

Possibly the most important change that you could bring to the workplace is a change of attitude. To reduce energy waste, people in the workplace must make energy conservation a priority. Once you get motivated, perhaps you can help motivate your fellow workers. Some ways to encourage energy conservation attitudes of others include:

- *setting a good example by turning off lights and machinery and by following suggested heating and cooling practices*
- *finding interesting posters or slogans about energy conservation to place around the building to remind others to save energy*
- *having an energy conservation meeting so everyone can contribute ideas that may help save money.*

## Cleaner environment

Companies in hospitality, travel and tourism are also very aware nowadays of the importance of a clean working environment for their workers. A clean working environment is concerned with:

- *the quality of the air that workers are breathing*
- *levels of pollution*
- *litter*
- *waste disposal.*

These types of issues are known as public health issues because they affect the health of everyone. Other public health policies that employers are concerned with include anti-alcohol regulations, lighting and **radiation** regulations. You will look at these later in this unit.

## • *Air quality and pollution* •

Since the late 1970s, there has been a steady increase in concern about the air quality in the workplace. It is now known that all sorts of **airborne contaminants** are present in the workplace and contribute to indoor pollution. Certainly many of these pollutants can affect the health of the people working in the buildings.

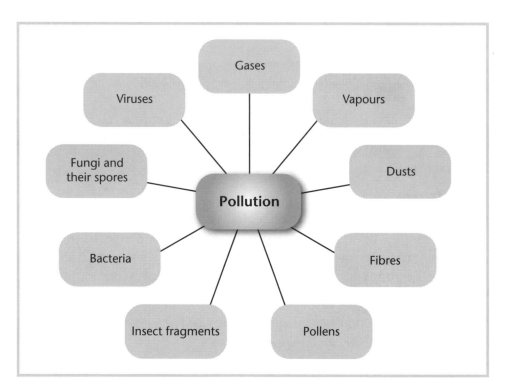

## GIVE IT A GO: the air you breathe

Work with a partner to check that you understand each of the different kinds of pollution. Which do you think exist in your college or school or, if you work part-time, your workplace?

## • *Workplace smoking policies* •

One particular source of airborne substances has become a point of real public interest – tobacco smoke. There are few topics of conversation more likely to stir emotion and create heated debate than the issue of cigarette smoking. Approximately 30 per cent of adults in the UK now smoke, which means that the other 70 per cent come into contact with smoke and are at risk of tobacco's side-effects. One of Britain's biggest pub chains, Wetherspoons recently announced plans to ban smoking in all its outlets by May 2006.

## CASE STUDY – A SMOKING POLICY

The Health and Safety Executive (HSE) has issued a booklet offering advice on passive smoking at work. It states that when smokers and non-smokers share the same room, non-smokers cannot avoid inhaling some of the smokers' tobacco smoke. This is '**passive** smoking'. The booklet also mentions that passive smoking can cause severe irritation to the eyes, throat and respiratory tract – your lungs in other words.

The HSE has therefore recommended that all employers should introduce a policy to control smoking in the workplace following full consultation with their employees. They go on to say that a policy on smoking should result in:

- a better, cleaner corporate image
- reduced conflict between smokers and non-smokers
- a reduction in staff turnover
- lower cleaning costs and less need for redecoration.

In some situations, a complete ban on smoking may be justified for safety reasons, for example where there is a risk of fire or explosion. However, in all other cases the HSE recommends that all employers should have a specific policy on smoking in the workplace. The policy should be written down and be generally available.

Some employers have already acted to ban smoking completely. Others have found success simply by allowing it. Buildings that are well **ventilated** can cope with a moderate amount of smoking.

Employers should make sure buildings are ventilated to protect their employees. Ignoring this issue brings serious risks for employers. They could face **prosecution** for poor air quality.

- Is it against the law to smoke anywhere at work?
- What is passive smoking?

### GLOSSARY

**Passive** means that something is being done to you and you have no choice in the matter.
**Ventilated** means that a constant supply of fresh air enters a building.
**Prosecution** means taking legal action against someone.

# Health and hygiene relating to work

It is vital that all staff work together to maintain a clean and healthy environment.

Cleanliness is important for all staff in hospitality, travel and tourism – your hair, skin, teeth, hands and nails should be washed regularly and kept clean. You have already considered the importance of personal cleanliness and hygiene for all chefs and food handlers in Unit 1.

The correct technique for washing hands effectively is shown in the drawings below.

**1** Rinse your hands under warm running water and then lather with about a teaspoon of soap.

**2** Wash all the surfaces of your hands and fingers for at least 10 seconds. It is easy to miss backs of hands and under nails.

**3** Rinse your hands thoroughly to wash off all soap and dirt.

**4** Dry your hands using a paper towel or an air dryer.

▲ **Procedure for washing hands**

 **WHAT if?**

## ... *you noticed a hygiene problem at work?*

Imagine that you are working as a sales consultant in a high street retail travel agency. Recently one of your colleagues has started to arrive for work looking a little scruffy and smelling a fair bit. Why does it matter? What would you do about it?

## ● *General healthcare policies* ●

An organisation should provide healthcare policies that explain their approach to health and hygiene in the workplace.

These will usually include anti-alcohol regulations, as drinking alcohol stops you from being able to carry out work efficiently and safely at work.

General healthcare policies for employees may include providing a company nurse or doctor who you can consult for work-related health problems. They might offer an annual flu jab service and regular work-place testing for common medical problems.

An employer might also offer employees private health insurance. This means that your employer pays a regular amount to an insurance scheme so that you can receive free treatment for occasional illnesses or emergencies. You may have to have a medical examination before joining the scheme. People with chronic health problems or who are smokers may not be allowed to join.

### GIVE IT A GO: healthcare benefits

Why do businesses provide workers with such healthcare benefits?

# Transport alternatives

Car use is one of the biggest causes of pollution and has many negative effects on the environment:

- *Exhaust fumes pollute the air, contributing to diseases such as asthma.*
- *New roads built to deal with traffic congestion destroy wildlife habitats.*
- *Cars use up non-renewable energy resources, including **fossil fuels**, plastics, rubber and metals.*
- *Cars produce waste which contaminates the environment, including old batteries, used oil and tyres.*
- *Old, scrapped cars contribute to waste disposal problems.*

### GLOSSARY

**Fossil fuels** result from the remains of ancient plant and animal life that have been transformed into coal, oil, and natural gas.

## ● *Getting to and from work* ●

One way that everyone can help the environment and conserve energy is by considering alternative methods for getting to and from work.

Many local authorities have transport policies that aim to reduce car use. This includes cycle lanes, park and ride schemes, and traffic calming in residential areas. Many people are now walking and cycling to their workplaces both to save on fuel and to gain valuable exercise. Given the slow movement of traffic due to congestion on the roads, cycling is one

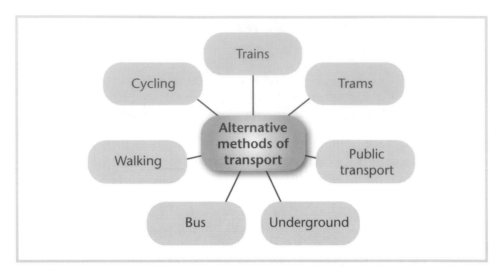

of the quickest ways to get around cities. If you have to travel by car to get to work, it may be possible to share the car with others. This will help cut down on costs and fuel usage.

## • *New developments in transport* •

Many towns and cities in the UK are now considering creative new methods of controlling traffic and transport problems, such as the use of congestion charges.

## CASE STUDY – LONDON CONGESTION CHARGE

**What?** The scheme encourages people to think again about using their vehicles in central London and to choose other forms of transport.

Motorists who want to travel in or through central London have to pay a daily charge.

**Why?** Before the scheme was introduced, traffic movement in central and inner London was severely hampered by congestion – the average speed was below three miles per hour. Transport for London says the charge will reduce congestion, improve the bus network, and make central London a more pleasant location for residents, visitors and businesses.

**How?** All vehicles driving across the £5 charge zone have to pay. However, some vehicles are exempt from the charge (e.g. taxis, licenced minicabs, emergency services, blue/orange badge holders, alternative energy vehicles). Others are entitled to a discount – mainly residents, but also some vehicle breakdown services.

**Where?** The 'boundary' of the zone is formed by the Inner Ring Road in London, on which there will be no charge to drive.

- Why has London decided to introduce the congestion charge scheme?
- How might tourism in London benefit if the charge is successful?
- What else might happen within the UK, if London's congestion charge works?

Other cities, such as Stratford-upon-Avon, Edinburgh, Dublin, Lincoln and York have converted their buses to use alternative fuels, such as Liquid Petroleum Gas (LPG), in order to help and promote more efficient fuel usage. LPG is economical because there is a **surplus** of it left over after oil refining and extracting gas.

> **GLOSSARY**
>
> **Surplus** is the amount left over after what is needed.

### EVIDENCE ACTIVITY

#### Your job and the environment

Discuss the environmental factors that are important to a chosen job role, such as that of a resort representative or tour guide.

# The law

## How the law helps you at work

Laws are designed to protect people and society from harm. They cover all areas of life and set out the punishments for those who harm others. As discussed in earlier units, there are many laws that affect the workplace and employment. Many of these laws have been developed and passed by the government to keep workers safe while they are at work.

Laws are made through Acts of Parliament. They are discussed and agreed by the House of Commons and the House of Lords. Sometimes laws are updated because of changing situations in society. The title of each Act shows whether it has been amended and gives the date it became law. The way law should be put into practice is often set out in Regulations, such as the National Minimum Wage Regulations 1999.

### GIVE IT A GO: laws in the UK

Working on your own or with a partner, make a list of the different aspects of the workplace that are covered by laws in the UK – think about the environment and conditions.

Every year in the UK many people are injured and killed in work-related accidents. In the year 2003/4, statistics showed:

- *235 workers were killed in work-related accidents.*
- *159,809 injuries were reported.*
- *9 million days were lost due to workplace injury.*
- *30 million days were lost due to work-related ill health.*

The three main causes of work-related injuries were:

- *injury while handling, lifting or carrying*
- *slipping, tripping or falling on the same level*
- *being struck by a moving (including flying/falling) object.*

The three main causes of **fatal** injuries were:

- *falling from a height*
- *being struck by a moving vehicle*
- *being struck by a moving (including flying/falling) object.*

**GLOSSARY**

**Fatal** means resulting in death

The vast majority of these accidents are avoidable. These statistics give an idea of just why health and safety is such an important issue in the workplace. As the hospitality, travel and tourism sector is one of the largest employers in this country, many of its workers are affected by accidents at work.

## Health and Safety at Work Act 1974

One of the most important pieces of legislation surrounding the workplace and the conditions that people work in is the Health and Safety at Work Act 1974.

This Act, which is also known as HASAWA, was passed with two main aims:

- *to protect all employers and employees*
- *to increase awareness of safety among people at work, both employers and employees.*

The Act states that an employer has a duty 'to ensure so far as is reasonably practicable, the health, safety and welfare at work of all his [or her] employees'. The law also requires every employee to:

- *take reasonable care of the health and safety of themselves and others*
- *co-operate with employer's arrangements for ensuring health and safety*
- *not interfere with or misuse anything provided in the interests of health, safety or welfare.*

It can be clearly seen that health and safety at work is everybody's responsibility. The Act also protects the members of the public who may be affected by the activities of those at work.

The Health and Safety Executive has been set up by the government to check that employers follow the law. It is responsible for investigating accidents at work and cases where health and safety regulations have been broken.

## ● *Responsibilities of the employer* ●

The employer's responsibilities are:

- ▣ *to provide and maintain premises and equipment that are safe and that aren't a risk to health*
- ▣ *provide supervision, information and training on health and safety matters*
- ▣ *produce a written statement of 'safety policy' for employees which includes how they intend to carry this out*
- ▣ *consult with the employees' safety representative and establish a Safety Committee.*

Regulations state that employers must also:

- ▣ *ensure that there is adequate ventilation*
- ▣ *maintain a suitable temperature, between 13–16°C depending on levels of physical activity*
- ▣ *provide suitable lighting to allow people to work safely*
- ▣ *provide rest facilities for workers to take regular breaks*
- ▣ *limit employees' working week to an average of 48 hours of work.*

▲ **All employers must display a health and safety law poster**

# Other laws affecting you at work

### • *European Union Directives on health and safety at work* •

These regulations cover a number of areas and issues as shown in the diagram below and work to support the HASAWA.

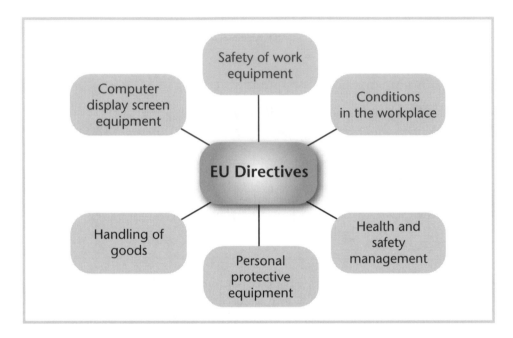

### • *VDU radiation policy* •

These regulations are especially important for retail travel agents or tour operators whose employees have to use computers and visual display units (VDUs) during their work. Employers must plan for and allow suitable breaks in any work that involves display screens and also provide information and training for all display screen users. Employees who are regularly using VDUs are entitled to free eye tests.

### • *Dangerous substances* •

In hospitality and catering especially, there are occasions when an employee might come into contact with dangerous substances and chemicals. For example, some hospitality staff will be in regular contact with cleaning materials such as bleach. Such chemicals can be very dangerous if not used correctly and should be used following the manufacturers instructions.

### • *Equal opportunities* •

There are a number of laws that ensure all people are treated equally. They protect the rights of all people to have the same opportunities at work.

- **Race discrimination** – *The Race Relations Act 1976 makes it unlawful to discriminate against or victimise anyone on the grounds of their colour, race, nationality, ethnic origins or national origins.*
- **Sex discrimination** – *Sex discrimination is where an individual is treated less favourably than another because of their gender. It also covers situations where a married person is treated less favourably than a single person. The test is whether the person would have received the same treatment but for his or her sex or marital status. This is covered by the Sex Discrimination Act 1975.*
- **Disability discrimination** – *The Disability Discrimination Act 1995 made it unlawful to directly discriminate against a person because of their disability. This law requires that all organisations ensure they are accessible to disabled people. Employers also have a duty to make sure the working environment does not disadvantage any disabled employee.*
- **Discrimination because of sexual orientation or religion or belief** – *It is now also illegal to discriminate on the grounds of a person's sexual orientation. This means that treating someone less favourably because of their sexuality is against the law, for example a straight employer discriminating against a gay employee or the other way round. Discrimination because of a person's religion or similar beliefs is also against the law. This is covered by the the Employment Equality (Religion or Belief) Regulations 2003.*

> **GLOSSARY**
>
> **Discrimination** means treating someone unfairly, for example in education, employment or business.

## The Equal Pay Act 1970

This covers male and females of any age, and gives them the right to the same pay and benefits for the same job or work that is proved to be of equal value. It is worth mentioning that in the UK the average woman's pay is still lower than a man's even with this legislation.

## The National Minimum Wage Act 1998

This law states that all workers over the compulsory school leaving age (16 years old) must be paid the National Minimum Wage.

From 1 October 2004 the rates were:

- *adult rate: (workers of 22 and over) £4.85 per hour*
- *development rate: (workers aged 18 to 21) £4.10 per hour*
- *young workers: (over 16) £3.00 per hour.*

▲ **Everyone is entitled to a minimum wage**

## Data Protection Act 1998

This Act protects people's rights over information that companies and individuals hold on them. The Act requires companies and individuals who process and keep information about their customers to tell the customer how the information will be used. This covers information stored on a computer and also paper-based records, such as any ordered filing system.

## EVIDENCE ACTIVITY

### Which laws are the most important?

1 Describe the laws that are important to one particular job, such as that of bar person in a pub or customer service agent in an airport.

2 Explain why you think some work-related laws may be more important than others.

Check your understanding of the information in this unit by answering the following questions. Then find the answers in the wordsearch.

1 What is the term used to describe the area, place and general surroundings that people work in? (11)

2 If a company encourages its staff to save energy, it is said to be helping ................... energy. (8)

3 What is the device that regulates temperature in rooms or on equipment called? (10)

4 Which major pub chain has recently announced a ban on smoking in its public houses? (12)

5 What is the word that means packaging is made to breakdown and dissolve after it has been thrown away? (13)

6 One alternative way that staff could use to get themselves to work other than driving. (7)

7 The Health and Safety Executive is often referred to as the ................... (3)

8 If people are treated unfairly within the workplace, it is called ................... (14)

9 A law that affects both employers' and employee's safety in the workplace. (6)

10 The ................... is the lowest amount of money that people working in the UK should be paid. (8, 7, 4)

```
B D J E C K Q T T T O W E N H T D E E C
C I E L V Z R K H M P J O Z A K V G E Z
D D O L X L L E F P U I R H M C Z A O D
T G I D V P R S Q X T U J H B Z V W A X
X B N S E M C T L A X S Q E T D Q M F E
U I O I O G N C N P G A J N C X U U P M
T M C S L I R I K C Q W Z V G T O M S O
N O T I I C M A M C T A C I B S A I E Q
D A M T H I Y X D E Z S Z R Z R M N U Y
T Y Q O R B O C B A R A Z O F A F I L I
Q B F C A Q W M L D B H N N G Z Z M L F
H W S E V R E S N O C L T M R X G L A W
S I Y X M F Q L J K V D E E Q M Y A V W
D J T E Q X A B G Q J R V N V J G N N O
A W A G L K K J O A B I K T Q X S O M W
D U K D Y R E T E L O F M O N B F I R F
R G N C R S H L L G N C W A G S O T J G
H W E T H E R S P O O N S Z C U X A P B
D U M Y V P M A R D Y P R V T U O N Y F
F A M C F F T B H O G D J J X H D R L O
```

# unit 6

## Financial management

This unit will provide you with the knowledge and confidence to manage your money by looking at how money is earned and developing personal budgeting skills. You will look at how you spend your money and which financial services you can choose from.

*In this unit you will learn about:*

▭ sources of income
▭ managing personal finance
▭ the importance of keeping a personal budget.

## Sources of income

### At work

Most people who work are employed by someone else – an individual or an organisation. They are an employee.

#### ● *Gross income* ●

Employees receive their pay on a regular basis, normally weekly or monthly. Their pay will include the basic wage, plus any **overtime** payments and bonuses. This is the 'gross income'. However, this is not the amount that you will actually be paid!

#### ● *Deductions* ●

The money actually received by the employee is the money earned, less the following deductions:

1   Compulsory contributions – payments that you must make:

- National Insurance (NI) – a payment made to the government to allow them to provide financial assistance to workers if they are off work due to sickness or they become unemployed. It also covers the payment of the basic state pension.

- Income Tax – a payment made to the government to pay for nationally funded services and projects, such as the army, navy and air force, schools and colleges, and the civil service.

2   Optional contributions – payments that you choose to make:

- Pension/superannuation – payments into an investment fund, as a savings plan for you to receive regular payments when you retire from work.

- Union subscription – payments made to unions, in return for which the union will represent you at work and negotiate better working conditions and benefits with your employer on your behalf.

- Charitable donations – a regular payment made, if you wish, to a charity of your choice, such as Cancer UK, Anthony Nolan Bone Marrow Trust, Royal Society for the Protection of Birds (RSPB).

## • *Net income* •

The payment that employees actually receive is called their 'net income'. The employer has the responsibility of calculating the **mandatory** contributions and making those payments to the government. This is called PAYE – Pay As You Earn – when your tax is paid via the payroll department, before you receive any money.

Here is an example of a payslip, where the employee is paid monthly:

| Employee name Silvia Ruiz<br>Employee number    0001234<br>Pay date May    2005 | | | | Company name<br>**Happy Days Travel** |
|---|---|---|---|---|
| **Pay and Allowances** | | **Deductions** | | **Balance/net pay** |
| Base pay | 807.67 | NI | 64.94 | £611.67 |
| Overtime | 49.11 | PAYE | 177.39 | |
| Incentives | 40.00 | Pension | 37.45 | |
| | | Union | 5.33 | |
| Total | 896.78 | Total | 285.11 | |

▲ **Example payslip**

## ● *Self-employed people* ●

People who are self-employed work for themselves. They must also pay income tax and National Insurance. This is generally paid annually at the end of the tax year. They must keep accurate financial records so that the tax they owe can be calculated. This includes records of:

◻ *the money paid to them*
◻ *the costs they have incurred (that is the money they have spent), e.g. buying stationery, tools, business phone calls*
◻ *the salary of any staff.*

Most self-employed people hire an accountant to check their figures to ensure that the information given to the tax office is correct.

## ● *Freelance workers* ●

Individuals who are self-employed may work freelance for other organisations. This means that they are free to work for more than one organisation at a time. They are also known as contractors as they sometimes negotiate short-term contracts with employers. Although they are usually paid higher rates than regular employees, they may be out of work for periods of time between contracts.

## GIVE IT A GO: types of employment

State whether the following individuals are employed, self-employed or freelance workers.

- Sarah works permanently for a major high street travel agency.
- Paul is a tour guide. He agrees the set period of time he will work for different tour operators, escorting groups of holiday makers around different countries.
- Winston has his own small business, selling designer coffees from a cart in the high street of a busy market town.
- Laura has worked as a customer service agent with British Airways at Heathrow airport for three years now.

▲ **Is Paul employed, self-employed or freelance?**

## EVIDENCE ACTIVITY  P2

### Sources of income

1 Working in pairs, produce a fictional payslip for an employee working in the hospitality, travel and tourism sector.

2 Decide what type of employee the payslip is for and what compulsory and optional contributions to include.

3 Design your payslip carefully so that all details are clear.

4 Write a short report to explain how the employee's income is made up.

5 Produce a display board to show all the information your class has produced.

---

**GLOSSARY**

**Interest** is the money people receive from their bank or building society, which has been made from investing their savings.

**GLOSSARY**

**Inherit** means to receive money, property, rank or a title when someone dies.

**GLOSSARY**

**A benefit** is an allowance paid by the government that people are entitled to because they are out of work, have a low income or are disabled or long-term sick.

# Other sources of income

### • *Interest from savings* •

When you have money in a bank or building society account, you will earn **interest** on your savings. The financial institution invests the money that customers have in their accounts and pays them a percentage of their savings as interest.

### • *Borrowed money* •

If you are working and want to buy an expensive item, such as a car, flat, house or music system, you may borrow the money needed to buy the item. You then pay back the value, plus interest, over an agreed timescale. The money you borrow to buy your house is called a mortgage. You can borrow money on a credit card, which you will look at later in the unit. Many high street shops now offer their customers the opportunity to have a store card, which is similar to a credit card.

### • *Inherited money* •

People sometimes **inherit** money when a relative or friend dies and leaves them money in their will. You have to pay tax on money that is inherited when the value is more than £263,000. This includes the value of gifts made in the seven years before the person died.

### • *Allowances and benefits* •

The UK government pays benefits to people on low wages.

**Housing benefit** – If you are managing on a low income, you may be entitled to housing benefit. This helps pay your rent. When calculating your benefit, local councils will look at:

- *your income*
- *your savings*
- *your partner's financial situation*
- *your circumstances, e.g. your age and family situation, whether you have any children, whether you or any of your family are disabled.*

**Council tax benefit** – You can also claim this benefit if you are on a low income. Your local council will calculate it using the same information as for housing benefit.

# Out of work benefits

The government also makes payments to people who are out of work, but who are looking for employment. They may be entitled to housing benefit and council tax benefit, which you have just looked at.

### ● *Jobseeker's allowance* ●

Jobseeker's allowance, also known as JSA, is the main benefit for people who are out of a job. This provides money for their living expenses while they are looking for a job. You usually need to be aged over 18 to receive JSA. You are asked to actively demonstrate that you are looking for work while you receive this benefit. There are two kinds of allowance:

- ***contributory*** – *this is based on your National Insurance contributions from previous jobs*
- ***means tested*** – *this replaces income support. It is based on income and takes into consideration whether you have a partner who is working and whether you have any savings.*

If you are aged 16 or 17 you are unlikely to have worked for long enough and paid enough NI contributions to get contribution-based JSA. You may be able to get income-based JSA for a short period in special circumstances. For example:

- *you are forced to live away from your parents*
- *you will suffer severe hardship if you do not get JSA*
- *you are a member of a couple who has responsibility for a child.*

### ● *Income support* ●

This money is available for people aged under 60 who are on a low income. People aged 60 or over can claim Minimum Income Guarantee.

You may qualify for Income Support if you are:

▭ *aged between 16 and 59*
▭ *on a low income, and*
▭ *either not working*
▭ *or working on average less than 16 hours.*

If you have to attend your Jobcentre regularly, you cannot get Income Support.

### • Child benefit •

This is a benefit for anyone bringing up children and is paid for each child aged under 16. It is not affected by income or savings. You can also claim child benefit if your child:

▭ *is aged under 19 and studying full-time*
▭ *is aged 16 or 17 and has left school recently, and has registered for work or training with the Careers Service or Connexions Service.*

### • Working tax credit •

This is another benefit available to people who have one or more children. It aims to support working families on low incomes. You can claim it if you work an average of 16 hours or more a week. You get more money if you work over 30 hours a week. How much you get depends on your circumstances.

## EVIDENCE ACTIVITY  P1

### Benefits

Working in small groups, find out more about the six benefits listed below:

- housing benefit
- income support
- council tax benefit
- jobseeker's allowance
- child benefit
- working tax credit.

Visit your local Job Centre and research on the Internet. Present your findings to the rest of the class.

# Managing personal finance

## Attitudes to work and money

We are all individuals so we each like to spend our money on different things. Some people prefer to have money in their bank account and will regularly save some of their salary. Others spend all of their salary every month on going out, eating and drinking, buying clothes, visiting the cinema and the theatre, and enjoying regular holidays. They may have a more **flamboyant** lifestyle. Some of us like the excitement of gambling and trying to win more money to spend.

> **GLOSSARY**
>
> **Flamboyant** means colourful, exciting and attention grabbing.

### CASE STUDY – DIFFERENT ATTITUDES

Alton and Luke are both 19 years old and work together as sales consultants in a busy travel agency.

Luke likes to live life to the full. He often goes out with his friends to bars and nightclubs. He likes to drive his car, which he bought by getting a loan for the full amount. He regularly buys new clothes and has store cards for three popular fashion stores. He has money outstanding on each card. Luke lives with his parents and spends all his money on himself and he sometimes puts a bet on the horses. However, he has not won anything yet. He buys a lottery ticket every weekend and knows exactly what he will spend the money on if he wins! Luke has agreed an **overdraft** with his bank, which he has now spent.

Alton is careful with his money; each month he gives an amount to his mother for rent and puts at least £50 into his building society account. He normally only goes out with his friends at the weekend and works part time in a local pub two nights every week to save up for his first car.

> **GLOSSARY**
>
> An **overdraft** is a temporary loan arrangement on your bank account for when there isn't enough money in the account to cover all your bills.

- Identify where Luke is being reckless with money and where Alton is being careful.
- What are the consequences for each?

### GIVE IT A GO: spending habits

Discuss in small groups what your own spending habits are. Do you save or spend?

# Using banks, building societies and post offices

There are many different types of organisations providing services to help you save money, including banks, building societies, and the Post Office. Most of these organisations offer you different types of service. You can visit the organisation by going to the local branch and speaking to someone face to face or have a telephone account where all contact with your bank is made by telephone. Completing all your **transactions** by Internet banking is becoming popular as it is a very convenient way of managing your personal finance. You can transfer money out of your account and pay bills by giving typed instructions on your bank's web pages. You have instant access to check the up-to-date information about your account, such as how much you have in it and to view the most recent transactions.

▲ Internet banking is becoming popular

▲ Some customers prefer face-to-face contact

## • *Saving schemes* •

Individual Saving Accounts (ISAs) are an easy and tax-free way to save and invest. The government introduced them to encourage people to get into the habit of saving. They currently allow you to save up to £7000 a year. You can save into an ISA account on a monthly basis. There are many types of savings schemes available to suit all income levels. Other examples are National Savings and Post Office Savings Accounts. You can get advice on ISAs from your bank. An independent financial advisor can look at your income, savings and expenditure and give you advice on the best savings scheme for you.

## • *Loans* •

A loan is an agreement between you and a financial organisation that lends you an amount of money. You must repay the value of the loan over an agreed period of time plus an extra amount of money, which is called the interest on the loan. There are many companies offering a wide range of deals on loans and there is lots of competition, so it is important to shop around to get the best deal.

# Running a bank or building society account

When you open a current account, you are offered a variety of services to help you run your personal finances. Banks offer you several methods of paying for goods and services that you have purchased.

## ● *Payment cards* ●

There are different kinds of payment cards available:

▲ Some of the many cards available

- **Debit card** – *This takes money directly from your bank account, so you can only spend up to the amount in your account. Your debit card will show your card number, bank sort code, card issue number, your name and the expiry date. There may be a security hologram. There is usually a maximum amount of money that you can withdraw from your account in any one day.*
- **Credit card** – *This allows you to make payments when you buy goods. You are then sent a bill at the end of each month. You can spend up to the limit agreed with your credit card company, for example £1000. You do not have to pay the full amount of the bill each month. You can make a minimum payment only, if you like. However, interest is charged every month, on any money that you have not yet paid back.*

## ● *Using a cheque book* ●

With some bank and building society accounts you may have a cheque book. This allows you to write a cheque to pay for goods against the money you have in your account. If you write a cheque for more money than is in your bank account, your bank may 'bounce' the cheque. That means that payment will not be made and you may have to pay a charge to your bank.

A cheque book usually comes with a cheque guarantee card. This means your bank agrees to guarantee the payment on your cheques up to a limited amount, for example £50. Some organisations may not always accept a personal cheque for large amounts of money.

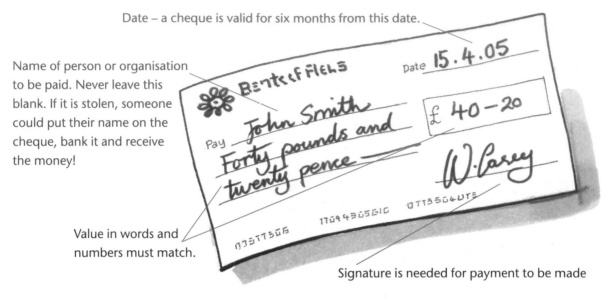

Date – a cheque is valid for six months from this date.

Name of person or organisation to be paid. Never leave this blank. If it is stolen, someone could put their name on the cheque, bank it and receive the money!

Value in words and numbers must match.

Signature is needed for payment to be made

▲ **Example of a cheque**

### ● *Personal finance records* ●

To help customers keep a record of their finances, banks and credit card companies send out a statement every month. This details money paid in as well as money spent. Building societies provide their customers with an account passbook, which is updated with each payment and withdrawal as they are made.

## EVIDENCE ACTIVITY (P3)

### *The best deal?*

In a small group, identify different organisations that you could use to invest your savings, including face-to-face, telephone and Internet banking. Allocate a different organisation to each person. Investigate that organisation to find out:

- what help it provides
- the different types of account it offers
- the range of loans available.

Make a display to show your information and prepare a short talk to give to everyone in your group.

# Personal budget

To budget is to estimate or plan your finances. That is, to calculate how much money you will earn and what essential items you must pay for, such as rent, food, bills and daily travel costs. This allows you to calculate how much **disposable income** you have for holidays, leisure activities and going out with your friends.

> **GLOSSARY**
>
> **Disposable income** is the amount of money that is left when we have paid for necessities.

## EVIDENCE ACTIVITY  P5

### Why should we budget?

1 In small groups, make a list of all the benefits of keeping to a budget.

2 List the problems you may have if you do not keep a careful check on your money.

## EVIDENCE ACTIVITY P3 P4

### Your budget

1 Make a note of how much money your income is in one month, from earnings and other sources.

2 List the costs of essential items you spend money on every month.

3 List the approximate value of non-essential items you buy every month.

4 Write down the answers to the following questions:

  a Are you spending within your budget?

  b What items could you do without or spend less on?

  c How much are you able to save every month?

5 Write a plan for your budget for the next two months. Make sure that you do not overspend.

## EVIDENCE ACTIVITY P6

### Creating a spreadsheet

Work with your information technology teacher to create a spreadsheet to record your income and all the money you spend.

| A | C | G | W | J | M |
|---|---|---|---|---|---|
| B | E | Z | O | K | V |
| S | E | A | R | C | H |
| R | F | I | D | L | O |

Check your understanding of the information in this unit by answering the following questions. Then find the answers in the wordsearch.

**1** What is the name given to a worker who is employed on a permanent basis by an organisation? (8)

**2** This is a mandatory contribution made from a person's salary. (8,9)

**3** This payment card may encourage you to spend more money than you can afford to. (6,4)

**4** We do this when we estimate or plan our finances. (6)

**5** This type of organisation is where many people save their money. (4)

**6** Something we should all do a little of every month! (4)

**7** This is the name given to the money we are paid. (6)

**8** The name of the piece of paper that details the money we have earned. (7)

**9** The name given to the monthly paperwork that your bank may send you to advise what money has gone in, or left, your account. (9)

**10** The word given to contributions that must be made from the money you have earned. (9)

```
P C D J B K G Q G B V C R M I F S
P A S R F Q K U Y U Q O T F B D M
K O Y P A S M R N D A W N U K H P
J R E S A C O T H G Y G E Y U L D
U G J L L T T E R E K V M O L A L
P Y A Y A I T I V T U F E U J S S
D R F D R G P D D A K X T P P A I
Y R N G K H T H O E S Z A I D Z J
K A E M P L O Y E E R H T L K H W
M H K F Y K N A B W N C S M I G Y
V R E S A O F L P H I O X I M Q Q
E C N A R U S N I L A N O I T A N
P N E F O Q D T V M R Z Y F W S F
D W J H D N U J A Q I E G E H X W
H F K T T A W Z L X L R L U H V C
U X O I A P O K V F U T Z G K D J
Y B Z Q B H B M J C M V W E P M Z
```

# unit 7

## The aspiring chef

The role of chef is an enjoyable and varied one. This unit aims to encourage and develop your enthusiasm for this area of work. The unit will introduce you to a range of food preparation and cooking skills. You will learn about and use a variety of different commodities and you will be encouraged to broaden your awareness of ingredients and methods. Your skills will be developed in the safe and correct use of knives. You will also learn about the correct use of equipment, commodities and methods of food preparation and cooking. You will study the importance and correct methods of cleaning work areas and equipment and develop a greater understanding of professional, safe and hygienic practices in the kitchen. This is a unit with a high level of practical content and you will need to demonstrate specific skills to your tutors and assessors.

Links to websites you may find useful when completing this unit are available through www.heinemann.co.uk/hotlinks (express code 6312P, then go to Unit 7).

*In this unit you will learn about:*

- equipment and commodities for food preparation and cooking
- safe and effective knife skills
- how to prepare, cook and present a range of dishes
- following professional, safe and hygienic kitchen practices
- how to clean equipment and work areas throughout the kitchen.

# Equipment and commodities

## Equipment

Any good kitchen is full of well-maintained and appropriate equipment. Professional chefs need a wide variety of equipment if they are to perform their roles to the best of their abilities.

Professional chefs rely heavily on their equipment. Equipment also needs to be looked after carefully. For example, if knives are blunt, they are no use.

### • *Safety and kitchen equipment* •

Safety is a major issue in the use of kitchen equipment. Much of the equipment used in professional kitchens is sharp, electric, hot and heavy or any combination of all of these. It must be treated and used with respect.

▲ **Professional chefs need a variety of equipment**

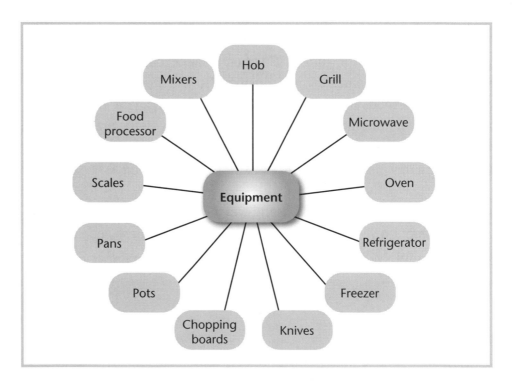

## GIVE IT A GO: equipment

Are there any pieces of this equipment that you have used or are familiar with? With a partner, discuss what each piece of equipment is and what it is used for. Check with your tutor if necessary.

In a busy kitchen everyone is responsible for the health and safety of themselves and other people around them. Anyone working in a kitchen must understand the importance of basic safety rules and follow them correctly. These general rules include:

- *staff must be adequately trained to operate any equipment that they may use*
- *notices should be clearly displayed explaining the operation of all equipment*
- *never store anything else on top of equipment*
- *never store equipment where it cannot be easily reached*
- *clean all equipment regularly and ensure that it is well maintained*
- *switch off all fuel and energy supplies (e.g. electricity) when equipment is not in use*
- *ensure there is sufficient space and ventilation when using equipment.*

## THINK ABOUT IT

Why are these rules important and why should they be followed by all kitchen staff?

## EVIDENCE ACTIVITY    P1

### The basics – equipment

Think about the cooking equipment in a well-equipped professional kitchen. Produce a list of 20 items of equipment, which could be used as an induction or training aid for a new chef. Explain how this equipment should be used safely. Prepare the list in an appropriate, professional IT format.

# Commodities

Commodities are the foods and food products used in a kitchen. A professional chef needs to be able to produce a wide range of dishes, including those from around the world. This requires a good knowledge and understanding of a wide range of commodities.

## GIVE IT A GO: the basics – commodities

List 15 different commodities that you think would be needed in a professional kitchen and explain what the items would be used for.

### ● *Meat and fish* ●

The main types of meat are beef, lamb, pork and bacon, and poultry and game. Poultry refers to all fowl that are reared for food, such as chicken, turkey, goose and duck. Game refers to wild animals and birds that are suitable for food, such as venison (deer) and pheasant.

Lean meat, which contains little fat, comes from young animals. As the animal's muscles have not had time to develop and become tough, lean meat is tender. Different quality of meat is obtained depending where it is from on the animal. This is known as the 'cut of meat'. To ensure that you get good results, you need to understand the different techniques that are used for cooking different cuts. You will think about this in the case study on page 146.

Meat is used for a wide variety of starters, such as pâtés, and main courses, for example grilled, roasted, in casseroles and stews. Meat and animal bones are also used to make sauces and stocks, although it is becoming common for establishments to purchase these ready-made. This is partly because of the time involved and also because of food safety issues. Meat sauces and stocks are ideal breeding grounds for bacteria and so great care is needed when they are being used.

When working with any form of meat, cooked or raw, good hygiene is absolutely essential to prevent any bacteria from causing food poisoning. Raw and cooked meat must always be stored apart – ideally in separate refrigerators.

▲ A range of raw meats

There is a massive variety of fish available, all of which make for excellent cooking. Fish is divided into two main groups:

🔹 *Oily fish – In oily fish, the natural oils are distributed throughout the body. The oil has a high **nutritional content** as it contains, for example, vitamins A and D. Examples are salmon, mackerel, herring, tuna and trout.*

● ***White fish*** *– The oil is only found in the fish's liver, so the flesh is white. Examples are cod, haddock, plaice and turbot.*

Fish can be further grouped by their shape into flat or round fish. Plaice, for instance, are white but they are also flat fish. Salmon are both oily and round.

Shellfish is another category of food we get from the sea. Examples are lobster, prawns, oysters, cockles and mussels.

Fish is available fresh but also comes in many different preserved forms. It can be frozen, smoked, tinned, pickled, in jars, dried, vacuum-packed and more. It is extremely versatile and provides chefs with a huge range of cooking options. As with meats, great care must be taken when handling raw fish or seafood of any kind. Fresh fish breaks down rapidly. It must be kept as close to freezing as possible until it is used. If you think that the fish you are preparing is not absolutely fresh, then you should not use it.

## EVIDENCE ACTIVITY    P3    M1    M2    D1

### Researching recipes

You are instructed by your Head Chef to come up with some recipes!

1 Working with a partner, research some dishes that would be appropriate on a modern restaurant menu.

2 Find a cookery method and finished dish for:

- three kinds of meat
- three kinds of fish
- three kinds of vegetables.

3 For each dish prepare a recipe for four people, with a method sheet that details how each dish should be prepared.

4 Discuss your suggestions with the rest of your group.

5 It may be possible to cook some of the dishes during your practical sessions. Prepare an evaluation sheet so that you can record your views on:

- how well the preparation went
- the problems you encountered
- how the final dish looked and tasted.

## • *Fruit and vegetables* •

Nowadays a great variety of fruit and vegetables is taken for granted all year round, due largely to modern production methods and the speed of transportation from all parts of the world. As with fish, fruit and vegetables are also available fresh and in a wide range of preserved forms, including frozen, tinned, in jars, dried and vacuum-packed. There is an almost endless array of fruit and vegetables, combined with different ways to prepare them, that chefs can choose from. The following menus show just a few examples of traditional British usage of vegetables and fruit as well as modern uses of tropical produce from around the world.

---

*Menu*

**Casserole of Highland Venison**
*cooked with Root Vegetables, Juniper & Red Wine*

---

**Grilled Fillet of Pork**
*with Braised Red Cabbage & Apple
and Potato & Celeriac Mash*

---

**Pot Roasted Chicken**
*with Buttered Carrots and Roasted Parsnips*

---

**Bramley Apple and Cinnamon Pie**

▲ **Traditional menu using fruit and vegetables**

---

··· m e n u ···

**Spiced Cumin and Coriander Lamb**
with Cinnamon Yam Mash

···

**Honey and Citrus Glazed Chicken**
with a Mango-papaya sauce and Coconut Rice

···

**Kumquat Chicken Oriental**
with Crisp Fried Noodles

• • •

▲ **Modern menu using fruit and vegetables**

---

## GIVE IT A GO: fruits and vegetables

List five fruits and five vegetables. Research the different ways that each can be prepared and served, and which area of the world each comes from.

## • *Dairy produce* •

This category refers to milk and the wide range of products that can be made from it.

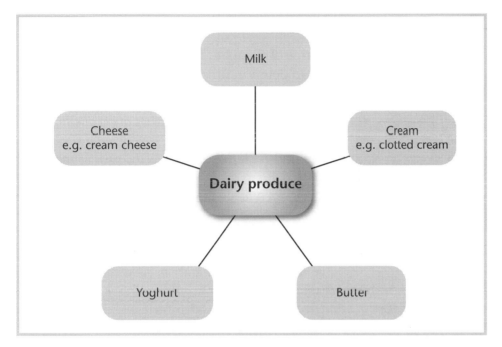

## GIVE IT A GO: dairy produce

Visit a local supermarket and make a list of all of the types of dairy produce that are available. Research five dishes that could be prepared using dairy produce as one of the main ingredients. Again it may be possible for you to prepare and produce some of these dishes with your tutors.

## • *Dry goods* •

This category covers beans, pulses such as lentils, rice and pasta. These are popular menu items in there own right, such as in a mixed bean salad, and as a part of a dish, such as in chilli con carne. Dried goods are preserved by having moisture removed from them. Before they are used by chefs they need to be **reconstituted**. Planning is important here. In the case of the kidney beans in chilli con carne, they would need to be soaked for 24 hours.

### GLOSSARY

**Reconstituted** means restoring the dried goods to their original state by adding water.

## GIVE IT A GO: dry goods

Find out about the range and uses of dry goods available. They are used in many different ways by many different cultures, for example a traditional use of peas in the UK is in the form of mushy peas!

## • *Preserving freshness* •

Many foods, such as vegetables and salads, arrive at the kitchen fresh. This provides the chef with the opportunity to use the food when it is at its best both in terms of quality and nutritional content. Fresh food must be stored carefully and used quickly to maintain these advantages.

▲ **Fish must be stored carefully**

Three of the main methods for stopping food from deteriorating rapidly are as follows:

▭ *Chilled foods – this means they should be delivered below 8°C. Foods that are kept chilled are those that bacteria can easily grow on if the food is not stored carefully and correctly, such as meat and fresh fish.*

▭ *Frozen food – is stored in freezers that operate at or below –18°C. The storage life of frozen food varies and depends on the initial state of the food, the quality of the freezer and how the food is stored in the freezer. The quality of some foods can be affected by freezing and some foods are not suitable to freeze. Great care should be taken not to refreeze food that has defrosted.*

▭ *Cooked food – has had much if not all of the harmful bacteria in it destroyed. Care must be taken not to re-contaminate the cooked food in any way and the food must be carefully stored and used within a safe time period. Cooked foods that are brought in to a premises will have a date stating when they must, by law, be used by.*

### GIVE IT A GO: preserving freshness

Write a list of six items of food in each of the categories frozen, or cooked or chilled.

As you saw in the sections on fish and fruit and vegetables, commodities may be preserved in other ways, including dried, tinned, bottled, vacuum-packed, freeze-dried, pickled, smoked, salted and more.

### GIVE IT A GO: preserved foods

Discuss all of the above terms and types of foods with your tutor to ensure that you have a good understanding of the range of foods and the differing ways in which they can be transported and stored.

Commodities that are preserved and stored in different ways provide the chef with an even greater range of foods. For example, fresh salmon is prepared, cooked and served very differently from smoked salmon. An important part of the chef's role is understanding these different types of commodity and how they are used.

Chefs must understand how to receive and store these foods correctly. If foods are stored incorrectly, this can lead to the growth of bacteria and ultimately to food poisoning. Inspect supplies on delivery and reject goods where necessary, for example leaking cartons. Mark goods with the delivery date and rotate stock to ensure that it is always used before it goes out of date.

▲ Salmon dish 1

▲ Salmon dish 2

## EVIDENCE ACTIVITY  P1

### *Planning a meal*

Imagine you are going to prepare an evening meal for 20 people.

1  Decide what starter, main course and dessert you will cook for them. You could look on the Internet to hep you find recipes.

2  Write a list of the equipment that you would need to cook it. Try to think of every item you would need. Make a note of any important safety points.

3  Create a list of ingredients for the meal, including what type of commodity each is, and any important points related to how they should be stored and used.

# Knife skills

All chefs need a range of knives if they are to prepare food effectively. Using a knife is a highly skilled part of the chef's job and one that requires constant attention to safety. In this section you will look at the range of knives that a professional chef uses and the skills a chef needs to develop.

## Knives

All knives must be treated with respect. They must be handled and used correctly, and care taken to ensure that they are always in good enough condition to allow the chef to do a professional job.

### THINK ABOUT IT

A knife that is blunt is more likely to cause an accident than one which is kept sharp. Why do you think this is true?

### ● *Knife safety rules* ●

The following knife safety rules should be followed at all times:

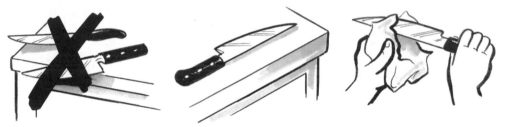

- *Always carry a knife with the point held downwards.*
- *Never leave knives with their edges or points sticking out over the edge of a table.*
- *Always concentrate when you are using knives.*
- *Always lay knives flat on a table so that the blade is not facing upwards.*
- *Always use the correct knife for the correct purpose.*
- *When you wipe a knife, ensure that the sharp edge of the blade is facing away from the hand.*
- *Never leave knives in a sink.*
- *Always ensure that the knife you are using is sharp.*
- *Keep the handle of the knife clean when you are using it so that it does not become slippery.*
- *Do not misuse your knives.*

Remember knives are an important tool for any chef but they can also be a serious workplace **hazard** if they are not used correctly.

### GLOSSARY

A **hazard** means a danger to all people in the working environment.

### ● *Different types of knives* ●

There are many different types of knives with a variety of sizes and blade shapes. These different knives are each designed for specific functions in the kitchen. Would you believe that there is even a special knife just for opening oysters?

## GIVE IT A GO: a basic set of knives

A basic set might consist of six knives. Study the table below and see if you can match the knife descriptions to the pictures.

| Type of knife | Used for |
| --- | --- |
| Small preparation knife 10 cm | General use, particularly peeling and preparing vegetables and fruit. Note: For the actual peeling of vegetables, some chefs prefer to use a vegetable peeler. |
| Medium-sized knife 15 cm | Slicing, shredding, chopping |
| Large knife 20 cm | Slicing, shredding, chopping |
| Flexible filleting knife 15 cm | Filleting fish |
| Palette knife | Spreading, lifting and turning items over |
| Boning knife 13 cm | Preparing and cutting up meat |

# Skills

There is a series of basic knife skills that any professional chef must perfect. These include peeling, chopping, dicing, shredding and slicing. These skills come with practice and you will have to practise during your practical sessions.

▲ **How to hold a knife**

An important starting point for knife skills is to learn to hold knives correctly. The photograph on page 139 illustrates the correct technique for holding a knife. You will notice:

- *The chef is holding the knife in her right hand with the fingers of her left hand firmly holding the lettuce to be shredded.*
- *The fingers of her left hand are tucked in to protect them from the knife blade.*
- *When she begins to use the knife, she will keep the flat blade pressed against the fingers of her left hand and make sure that the blade does not rise above the knuckles of her left hand.*

This technique will ensure that the sharp edge of the blade is always kept away from the chef's fingers. This might sound complicated but with practice this soon becomes second nature to a chef.

## ● *Sharpening knives* ●

A steel is the name given to the tool used by chefs to sharpen knives. Learning to use a steel effectively takes practice. A steel has a safety guard on the handle, so as to protect the chef's hands should the knife slip.

When using the steel you should draw the knife blade along the steel at a 45-degree angle, as shown in the photograph. This angle produces a sharp edge on the blade. This must be done on both sides of the blade.

There are a number of ways that the steel and knife can be held to sharpen knives. In your practical sessions you will learn about the most effective methods that can be used to sharpen knives.

▲ **Using a steel to sharpen a knife**

## ● *Using chopping boards* ●

Usually when a chef is using a knife, he or she is likely to be using a chopping board also. Using a chopping board helps to keep knives sharp, protects the work surface underneath and helps to maintain a clean, safe and professional work area. In days gone by all chopping boards were made of wood. Nowadays it is recognised that chopping boards made out of special plastic are far more hard-wearing and **hygienic**.

Plastic chopping boards are now available in different colours. This allows chefs to use one particular colour for raw meat and nothing else.

> **GLOSSARY**
>
> **Hygienic** means maintaining a clean condition, free from bacteria and other contamination.

**WHAT (if?)**

### ... *you were preparing ham sandwiches?*

What could happen if you had just finished cutting up a raw chicken on a chopping board, and then started to slice cooked ham for sandwiches on the same board?

Different colours are also available for other types of food such as fish, vegetables, dairy foods and so on. This means that chefs can keep foods separate and avoid something called cross-contamination. This is where harmful bacteria are transferred from one food to another during preparation or storage.

## GIVE IT A GO: board safety

Copy the table below and complete the missing gaps that show what each coloured board is designed for. Discuss this with your tutor to ensure that you have the correct usage for each colour.

| Colour of chopping board | Used for |
|---|---|
| Red | |
| Blue | |
| Green | |
| Brown | |
| Yellow | |
| White | |

## EVIDENCE ACTIVITY  P2

### Good practice

Produce a simple but effective word-processed document that will help inform any new member of the kitchen staff about:

- the dangers and safety issues when handling knives
- good practice in the use of chopping boards during food preparation.

# Prepare, cook and present food

Preparing, cooking and presenting food are three distinct stages that chefs undertake to ensure that their customers are provided with high quality food. If any of these stages goes wrong, it can have a disastrous effect on the final dish and the customer's impression of an organisation.

# Preparing food

Preparation is the key to good cooking and you will look at this stage next.

## WHAT if?

### ... you were making apple pies?

Imagine you were tasked with making apple pies by the Head Chef. What do you think you might need to do? Working with a partner, list the stages of preparation you would need to complete before putting the pies in the oven to cook.

### ● *Weighing and measuring* ●

Taking the example of the apple pie, if you were making it with fresh pastry you would certainly need to weigh out the ingredients for the pastry dough. Cooking is a profession which involves **precision** and accuracy. Being able to weigh out ingredients correctly in the right quantities is part of these skills. If a chef gets this part wrong, he or she might end up with pastry as hard as wood when the pie comes out of the oven. No amount of trying to make the apple pie look nice on the plate will alter the fact that the pastry is rock hard.

> **GLOSSARY**
>
> **Precision** means taking care to get something exactly correct.

### GIVE IT A GO: weighing out accurately

Using the Internet, find a recipe for short crust or sweet pastry. This is the type of pastry you might well use when making an apple pie. Weigh out the ingredients, following the quantities in the recipe. Then get a colleague or your tutor to double check the accuracy of your weighing out. You may discover just how easy it is to make mistakes at this stage!

### ● *Preparation methods and techniques* ●

There are other important preparation methods and techniques that you will need to practise as part of this unit.

▲ Grating

▲ Creaming

▲ Rubbing

▲ Folding

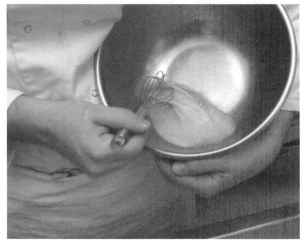

▲ Beating

▲ Stirring

▲ Mixing

▲ Seasoning

## GIVE IT A GO: preparation skills

Other skills you may need to use when preparing a dish include:

- grating
- creaming
- rubbing in
- folding

- beating
- stirring
- mixing
- seasoning.

What utensils or pieces of equipment are used for each skill? Give an example of a dish which requires use of this technique during preparation. Discuss all of these terms with your group and your tutor to ensure that you fully understand the meaning of each.

# Cooking food

When all the necessary preparation is complete, the chef will move onto the cooking stage of the process. During cooking food changes considerably. Cooking has many positive effects, such as changes in texture, colour and taste. The main reason, however, for cooking food is to ensure that it is safe to eat. All food has bacteria on it. As you have seen, some foods, particularly raw meat, can carry harmful bacteria, which can make you severely ill. Cooking, if carried out correctly, ensures that these bacteria are killed and the food is made safe to eat.

## GIVE IT A GO: why we cook food

Think about what would happen if we didn't cook our food at all. Write a list of the benefits that we get from cooking food.

You should have identified some of the following as other benefits that we get from cooking our food.

- It makes food more digestible – that is, easier to eat and break down in our stomachs.
- Cooking adds variety – think about all the different potato dishes, such as baked potatoes, roast potatoes, boiled potatoes, deep-fried chips, crisps and so on.
- It helps to make food more appetising. Who would fancy tucking into a plate of raw chicken?
- Cooking helps to thicken and set some foods, such as egg dishes.

There are many different techniques available to a chef to cook food. Choosing the correct cooking method for a specific food also improves **palatability** and ensures that the required texture and appearance of the finished dish is achieved. Some foods are more suited to some methods of cooking than others.

### GLOSSARY

**Palatability** means that the flavours in food are well developed and the food tastes nice.

## CASE STUDY – USING THE RIGHT CUT OF MEAT

A young chef, Alex, was asked by his Head Chef, Simon, to prepare and cook 20 portions of steak and kidney pie filling. Alex had made this once before. He was not really sure which meat to use because the last time it had already been diced up when it was given to him. He chose three whole fillet steaks from the meat fridge, diced them up and set about making the pie filling.

After the meat had been cooking on the stove for a couple of hours – he knew he had to do this to ensure that the meat became tender – the chef checked his pie filling to see how it was getting on.

He was amazed to discover that the only meat left visible in the sauce was the kidney. There did not appear to be any of the beef fillets he had carefully diced and added to the mixture.

When he told Simon what had happened, Simon hit the roof, 'What do you mean you've used fillet steak for steak and kidney pie!' he screamed.

Simon was very angry because Alex had used one of the most expensive cuts of steak. Fillet steak is a tender piece of meat that does not need a lot of cooking. Over the two hours that the mixture had been boiling on the stove the fillet steak had overcooked and disintegrated into the sauce!

So after several hours work, there was no pie filling – and three whole fillet steaks wasted.

- Who was more at fault here, Alex or Simon?
- What cut of meat should Alex have used to produce the steak and kidney pie filling?

## • *Methods of cooking* •

Chefs need to be familiar with all of the following methods of cooking. They also need to know which foods are suited to each method.

- *Boiling* – cooking in boiling liquid (for water this means 100°C).
- *Grilling* – cooking by direct heat from above or below, usually used for smaller cuts of meat, such as fillet steak (!) or fish.
- *Frying* – a quick method of cooking. Shallow frying is done on a pre-heated metal surface, or pan, with only a little fat. In deep-frying, food is immersed completely in very hot oil.
- *Roasting* – cooking with fat or oil in a preheated oven.
- *Baking* – dry cooking in a preheated oven, without any oil or fat.
- *Stewing* – the cooking of small pieces of tough or hard food in a minimum amount of liquid. Stewing usually takes place over a long period of time to help soften the food.
- *Poaching* – cooking in a liquid that is kept below boiling point. This is a gentle method of cookery suited to fish, eggs and certain types of vegetables.
- *Simmering* – cooking in a liquid that is kept just below boiling point, bubbling gently while it cooks.
- *Steaming* – cooking in steam.

To achieve this unit you will need to become competent in all of the above cooking methods. As with knife skills and preparation skills, practice will help you to become competent with these methods.

### ● *Seasoning and tasting* ●

Foods can be seasoned with salt and pepper, or flavoured with a variety of herbs and spices, to ensure that it tastes as good as possible. All foods should be tasted and tested before serving customers. After all, it is no good if the food looks good but tastes horrible! It is also important to test food to ensure that it is cooked sufficiently.

## Presenting food

While the majority of a chef's time is spent carefully preparing and cooking food, the customer, who will be eating the food, rarely sees any of this. The first they see of all of the hard work is usually when the food is placed in front of them by a member of the waiting staff.

If the food that is put before the customer looks horrible then all that hard work will have gone to waste. There is a saying that people 'eat with their eyes' and there is a lot of truth in this. It is essential that the food served to customers is presented in a way that looks attractive and appealing.

▲ **Food needs to look attractive and appealing**

It is during this final presentation stage that a chef can really show his or her skill and flair in making the food appear as attractive as possible. Colour combinations and a variety of techniques can be used to help with the presentation of the food. Chefs can use plates and serving dishes to help present the food attractively. How and where the food is placed on a plate also has an important part to play. Foods can be garnished in a variety of ways to help make the food look appealing. Chefs must be careful to avoid mess or spillages on the plate as these detract from the appearance of the dish.

▲ **Food can be made to look very appealing**

## EVIDENCE ACTIVITY  M2 D1

*Keeping a log of your skills*

Keep a log book of the dishes you prepare and cook while working towards this unit. You might find it useful to create a form like the one below to record your work. Ensure that you get your tutor or an assessor to sign your forms to agree that you have completed the work to the required standard. This record of your cookery work will help you look back and improve your skills.

You can use your logs to provide evidence of:

- a range of food preparation and cooking skills for different dishes  M2
- excellent and confident practical skills in a range of different food preparation and cooking situations.  D1

### Practical Evidence Sheet

| Candidate's name | | | |
|---|---|---|---|
| Evidence gathered in relation to Unit 7 The Aspiring Chef | | | |
| Date | Tasks undertaken | Skills demonstrated | Assessor's initials and comments |
| | | | |

# Working professionally, safely and hygienically

This section looks at professional working practices in the kitchen. You will think about professional standards of behaviour, including how to avoid hazards and ensure food safety.

## Professional

A kitchen is a busy and often pressurised place of work. Customers usually want their food served quickly and the kitchen soon becomes a hot and often frantic place during periods of service. In such an environment, surrounded by knives, hot pans, gas flames and the like, it is essential that chefs always act in a controlled and professional manner.

## ● *Working as a team* ●

A kitchen, like most organisations, will usually have a chain of command starting with the leader of the kitchen – usually referred to as the Head Chef. In larger kitchens there may well be different chefs for different roles. For example, there may be specific chefs who control the pastry section, the sauce section or the vegetable section. Even in smaller kitchens everyone will have their own roles and responsibilities. If it is all to come together ready for service, then the staff in the kitchen must work like a finely tuned machine in perfect harmony.

You may well have seen television shows set in professional kitchens, such as the celebrity chef Jamie Oliver's *Jamie's Kitchen*, where he took on 15 young trainees for a new restaurant, or Gordon Ramsey's *Hell's Kitchen*, where a group of minor celebrities had to work together to produce food for a busy restaurant. These kinds of programmes give a realistic view of the pressures of working in a busy kitchen.

Teamwork is essential in any professional kitchen. Listening is an important part of this. If a chef is not being attentive and misses an order or any instructions, it can quickly cause chaos.

## ● *Personal protective equipment* ●

Personal protective equipment (PPE as it is often known), is an important aspect of working in the hospitality industry. For both a chef and a member of the food service staff there are many dangers, as you have seen.

> **GLOSSARY**
>
> **Personal protective equipment** (PPE) are clothes and other items worn to protect against workplace hazards.

### GIVE IT A GO: What dangers?

Produce a list of all the possible dangers a chef might face while they are at work.

A chef may not need to wear protective goggles, helmets and gloves as someone working on a building site might, but there is still a need for protection. For example, the clothes the chef is wearing must protect from spillages and burns. If a chef worked in the clothes they had worn to get to work, the clothes would be heavily **contaminated** from the outside environment. There would be the danger that this contamination would be passed on to the food. The chef's PPE protects both the chef and the food.

> **GLOSSARY**
>
> **Contaminated** means to have become exposed to dirt, bacteria and other pollutants.

## GIVE IT A GO: a chef's clothes

1 For each item write why there is a need for that piece of clothing.

2 Think of any other benefits of chefs wearing a special set of clothing. Discuss your thoughts with a partner.

### ● *Managing time and working under pressure* ●

Part of being able to cope with working under pressure is good time management. Managing your time effectively involves working in a logical and ordered manner, so that all aspects of cooking are co-ordinated and come together to make the final dish. Imagine you have just cooked an order as simple as deep-fried cod. It is cooked to perfection, golden brown and crisp and ready to serve – then you realise you forgot to put the chips on!

All chefs need to learn to work in an organised way to avoid such things happening. Recipes should be followed. Some dishes are complex and even the slightest variation in the quantities and techniques will cause the final dish to fail. Hand in hand with this, chefs need to learn to work in a tidy way. It may be tempting to allow mess and rubbish to build up, thinking that you will clear it all away at the end of your cooking. However, if the area you are working in is not kept clean and tidy, it can quickly become an area of chaos where food is in danger of cross-contamination and you are constantly misplacing equipment.

## GIVE IT A GO: who do you want cooking your food?

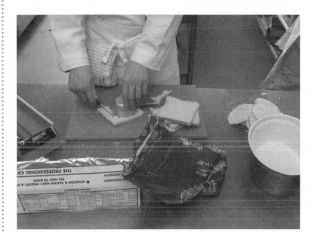

▲ Chef 1

▲ Chef 2

Look at the two photographs. Which chef do you think is likely to work more effectively and produce the best food?

## ● *Professional terminology* ●

Chefs also have to learn the **terminology** of the kitchen. This is the day-to-day vocabulary used by chefs to describe the food, the methods and the equipment they use in their role.

The concept of people going out for a meal cooked by professional chefs was developed into an art form in France. As a result a lot of the terminology used in the kitchen comes from France. For example, in Unit 2 you met the term *mise en place*. This means 'getting everything into place'. Chefs use this phrase to cover all of the work they do in preparation. For instance, the *mise en place* for making a tomato soup is the washing, peeling and chopping of all of the vegetables needed to make the soup.

### GLOSSARY

**Terminology** means the language, words and phrases associated with a particular topic, in this case professional cooking.

## GIVE IT A GO: researching terms

There are many French words that are part of the terminology of cooking. Working with a partner, use the Internet to research and produce a glossary of 20 of these commonly used terms. A few examples to get you started are:

*Au gratin* – cooked with breadcrumbs and/or cheese on top and lightly browned under a grill

*Béchamel* – white sauce made with milk, fat and flour

*Roux* – equal amounts of fat and flour bound together over heat. A roux is used to thicken sauces.

# Safety and hygiene

You have already looked at some important aspects of safety as you have worked through this unit, including the safe use of knives and storage of equipment.

Kitchens can be dangerous places. You must be constantly aware of other people and how your actions may affect them.

- *Always clear spillages up immediately.*
- *Dry slippery floors immediately. If this is not possible, put clear warning signs out.*
- *When handling hot objects always use suitable protection, such as a good quality, dry oven cloth.*
- *Never leave a deep fryer unattended when it is in use.*
- *Warn others of any dangers, such as hot pans.*
- *Never run or mess around in a kitchen – this is one of the biggest causes of accidents.*

## • *Electrical equipment* •

Electrical equipment that is not wired correctly presents a serious safety risk to anyone who touches that equipment. Bare wires or frayed cables must be reported immediately and the equipment should not be used.

There is an increased risk of injury if electrical appliances are allowed to come into contact with water. All kitchen staff must be vigilant to make sure that this does not happen. Sockets should be placed well away from any water source, such as a sink, to avoid such risks.

## • *Food safety and hygiene* •

Food hygiene relates to the good practices and procedures which ensure food is safe to eat. Good food hygiene covers every part of kitchen work from the delivery and storage of food, through preparation, cooking and serving. It is the responsibility – by law – of everyone involved in the food process. This includes chefs, food service staff, pot washers, managers, bar staff and anyone else who may come into contact with the food. These people are often referred to as food handlers.

The Food Safety Act 1990 is one of the main pieces of legislation that covers the handling of food. This law states that all food handlers must follow a strict code of practice. It also requires that adequate and appropriate training is given before anyone can handle food that is prepared for the general public.

Food handlers need to understand the areas shown in the spider diagram opposite.

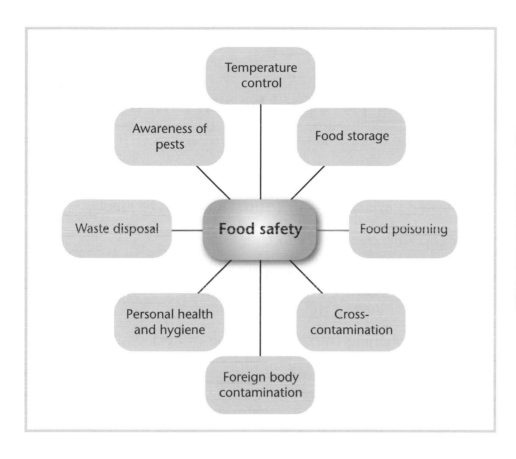

## ● *Food poisoning* ●

The main risk of poor food hygiene standards is an outbreak of food poisoning. Food poisoning is an acute illness caused by the consumption of contaminated food. The onset is sudden, normally within 1 to 36 hours, and it can last for up to seven days. The symptoms of food poisoning include stomach pains, fever, sickness, diarrhoea, vomiting and potentially even death.

The main causes of food poisoning are set out below.

- ▭ *Bacterial* – *for example, salmonella bacteria, which is commonly found in chickens and raw meats.*
- ▭ *Fungal* – *some moulds, yeasts and mushrooms produce poisons called mycotoxins.*
- ▭ *Chemical* – *for example, cleaning products such as bleach getting into the food can poison you.*
- ▭ *Metallic* – *not very common, but some metals such as lead can cause harm if they get into food. (In the past water pipes used to be made of lead!)*
- ▭ *Poisonous plants* – *for example, certain types of mushrooms are poisonous.*
- ▭ *Poisonous fish* – *there are certain fish and shellfish that are eaten and which have poisonous parts that must be carefully removed before eating.*

*• Food handler's good practice •*

## Rules for personal health and hygiene

- Maintain a good standard of personal body cleanliness.

- Keep hair clean and short or in a protective net.

- Always have clean hands and wash them regularly.

- Keep nails clean and short.

- Cover all cuts and sores with waterproof plasters.

- Do not smoke or spit near food.

- Avoid touching the face, ears, hair or neck while working with food.

- Do not work with food if you are suffering from serious health problems or such things as skin complaints and throat or nose infections.

- Wear clean and suitable protective clothing.

- Avoid wearing jewellery and perfumes or aftershave.

## CASE STUDY – FOOD POISONING

Danny is a commis chef in a busy hotel restaurant in South London. Over one summer weekend at Danny's hotel there was a wedding banquet for nearly 600 guests. In the run up to the wedding Danny had an upset stomach and had been suffering from sickness and diarrhoea. He had not let anyone know and he had carried on working to help prepare the food for the wedding. A lot of the time Danny had had to rush to the toilet and he had not always washed his hands after these visits.

Shortly after the wedding a number of complaints started to arrive at the hotel stating that many of the guests had fallen ill with sickness and diarrhoea.

1  What could be the possible outcomes for the hotel?

2  What might be the possible outcomes for Danny?

Make a list of your thoughts and discuss them with your partner.

## ● *Freezers and refrigerators* ●

Freezers and refrigerators are important pieces of equipment in any modern, professional kitchen. To ensure that they are used effectively and remain safe the following rules should always be followed.

- *Open the doors as little as possible in order to keep the temperature at the correct level.*
- *Keep all foods covered, wrapped or in appropriate containers to avoid any form of contamination.*
- *Always store raw meats at the bottom of a refrigerator.*
- *Do not overfill either the refrigerator or the freezer.*
- *Do not store strong-smelling foods, such as garlic, or dirty foods, such as unwashed cabbage, in the refrigerator.*
- *Check the temperatures of both pieces of equipment regularly.*
- *Regularly check the food stored in both and discard any that is unfit for use.*

### THINK ABOUT IT

Why is it important not to store any raw meats on the top shelf of a refrigerator?

Poor food hygiene standards may result in:

- *an outbreak of food poisoning*
- *loss of working days due to staff illness*
- *wastage of food*
- *loss of production and low efficiency*
- *prosecution and/or closure*
- *loss of custom due to poor reputation*
- *claims from the public for compensation.*

### THINK ABOUT IT

What do you think are the benefits of good hygiene standards?

## EVIDENCE ACTIVITY  P5  M3

### Dos and don'ts

1 Working with a partner, produce a list of rules that you think chefs should follow while they are working in a busy kitchen. Try to come up with a list of ten dos and don'ts that help a kitchen to run in a safe, professional and hygienic manner. Discuss these rules with your tutor and the rest of the group.

2 Produce a set of guidelines in a word-processed format that can be used during the induction of new employees in a kitchen environment.

3 Write an explanation about why it is so important for all kitchen staff to follow professional, safe and hygienic practices while at work.

# Clean equipment and work area

Maintaining a clean working area and equipment is an essential part of meeting food safety requirements. Cleaning removes matter that can support the growth of bacteria and pests, and reduces the risk of foreign body contamination in food being prepared. Staff morale can be enhanced by providing a more pleasing workplace.

## Methods

Basic methods of cleaning are set out below.

⊃ *Washing – to remove dirt, objects and debris using hot soapy water, for example from crockery, utensils and equipment. A dishwasher may be used.*

⊃ *Wiping – to remove debris and grease, using a cloth and ideally some type of **anti-bacterial agent**, for example from tables and trays. Cloths used to wipe down must always be clean themselves!*

⊃ *Sterilising – to kill all bacteria. This is used on specific items, such as cutlery or small items of machinery.*

A good system to follow for the cleaning of all items is as follows:

1 Pre-clean – to remove all loose debris and food particles.

2 Main clean – use hot soapy water (the water should be above 82°C to kill bacteria).

3 Rinse – to remove the soapy water.

> **GLOSSARY**
>
> An **anti-bacterial agent** is a product that kills bacteria.

4  **Disinfect** – to ensure the removal of all bacteria. This is best achieved by the use of hot, clean water.

5  Dry – best achieved by allowing the equipment to air-dry, in order to avoid re-contamination from cloths.

> **GLOSSARY**
>
> **Disinfection** is where bacteria is reduced to a level that presents no risk to the public.

## Equipment

Great care must be taken when cleaning knives and other equipment with sharp blades. Knives should never be left unattended in a sink as this may lead to injury to yourself or others. After cleaning, they should always be returned to their proper storage place.

Pots and pans should be cleaned thoroughly. Chopping boards are in regular, prolonged contact with food, both raw and cooked, and must be thoroughly cleaned, using the steps outlined above, to avoid cross-contamination. Scales and food processors also need careful cleaning to avoid cross-contamination.

## Work area

All work surfaces, whatever they are made of, must also be thoroughly and regularly cleaned. A chef should remember and stick to the saying 'Clean as you go'. All work surfaces must be cleaned using the steps discussed above. Any food material not used must be stored quickly and correctly to prevent any contamination or pest infestation. All food waste must be disposed of thoroughly and effectively. If food rubbish is allowed to be left out in a kitchen, it will quickly become a haven for any pests that can gain access to the food.

**EVIDENCE ACTIVITY**  **P4**

### A cleaning schedule

1  Produce a cleaning schedule that you think would be effective and appropriate for your workplace or college environment. Use the guidelines below to help you.

   • What should be cleaned?

   • When should it be cleaned?

   • What method should be used to clean it?

   • What safety precautions are needed?

   • Who should clean it?

   • Who is responsible for checking cleaning?

2  Discuss with your group and your tutor how effective your plan will be.

```
A C G W J M
B E Z O K V
S E A R C H
R F I D L O
```

Check your understanding of the information in this unit by answering the following questions. Then find the answers in the wordsearch.

**1** One item of equipment that you would expect to find in a modern kitchen is ........................ (8)

**2** This is the term for the clothing that you wear for protection from hazards while you work. (3)

**3** This is a popular type of fish. (6)

**4** Beans, pasta and rice are all examples of this kind of commodity. (3, 5)

**5** This is a rule that applies to a chef when he or she is using, carrying or washing knives. (2, 3, 6)

**6** If you chop raw chicken on a chopping board and then prepare ham sandwiches on the same one, there is a danger of this happening. (18)

**7** A cooking method which involves cooking over a long time to soften hard or tough foods. (7)

**8** A chef does this every day when he or she prepares everything that will be needed for cooking dishes for customers. (4, 2, 5)

**9** This is a white sauce that is made with milk, fat and flour. (8)

**10** The main reason that we cook our food is to ..................... (4, 8)

```
F W V I B U X P K N F R P Z R U X K
Q Q M I E E J J S D E E H L Y F W O
Z A B M C A T R U B C S X H R J M N
N P X G H R L Q I A P U J Y M E P Q
N F L K A M K S L J Q S H O O Z Q N
B T Z R M A D P O O H I K C G M I C
Z G J K E A N R I U S M E K J F Z L
N D E B L E I L Y T M T E P K W Z L
M F R U E N Z R E G W O Z T P W O X
I V A S O K M W E N O N Y W R N M U
N O I T A N I M A T N O C S S O R C
L M Y I L N F S J Q C D D Z Q X Y F
O L Q P G O O C N H V A Q S B N N J
P Z D V P A C Z G Z X R B D T O D O
K I N O M L A S A P I O M L X M A O
L V I V N F N H E I F N U W L R B V
H H Z Y I G Z J E R G K R M C I I W
S A U C E P A N E K K T J R H F K T
```

# unit 8

## Food service with a smile

The aim of this unit is to introduce you to the various skills needed to serve a range of foods in different food outlets. The unit is designed to stimulate your interest, enthusiasm and enjoyment for serving food to customers and will broaden your awareness of the care and skills required.

In this unit you will develop skills in dealing with customers and in handling utensils and equipment correctly. You will also learn how to clean utensils, equipment and the restaurant. As part of this unit you will develop your knowledge of professional, safe and hygienic restaurant practices.

*In this unit you will learn about:*

- how to prepare and maintain the food service area for a food service outlet
- how to deliver food and beverage service while demonstrating effective communication skills
- how to clear the food service area
- following professional, safe and hygienic kitchen practices.

# Preparation and maintenance

The food service staff must work in partnership with the chefs working on food preparation. These two areas cannot function without each other. Food service staff are responsible for preparing and maintaining the food service areas, so that food and beverages are served to customers in an efficient, safe and hygienic manner.

## Outlets

There are many different types of food outlet throughout the UK. Food service personnel might work in a restaurant, a café, a fast food outlet, such as McDonald's, or a coffee shop.

## Food service area

The food service area of most catering establishments will consist of two areas:

- *the customer area – which may be tables and chairs or simply bar stools, depending on the type of restaurant*
- *the service area – where the food and drinks are served from, which may include a counter or a dumb waiter.*

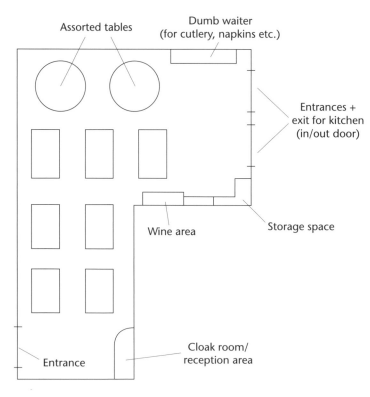

▲ **Possible layout of a food service area**

## GIVE IT A GO: a dumb waiter!

What is meant by the term 'dumb waiter'? Find out if your workplace or college has one and take a look at it.

If these areas are not kept clean, tidy and organised, it can create a serious hygiene risk, and no one will be keen to eat in a dirty or poorly maintained restaurant. As all waiting staff are food handlers, food safety and hygiene is vital and the principles you studied in Unit 7 apply in these areas also.

# Service equipment and service items

Food service staff need to prepare and maintain a variety of specialist equipment for their work.

To ensure that food is kept safe, hot and cold foods need to be kept at the correct temperature before they are served to a customer. Refrigerated units and heated units are used for this purpose. These units should be fitted with special thermometers that allow staff to monitor the temperature.

It is not only because of food safety that such equipment is needed. Food is more appetising when it is served at the correct temperature. For example, cold chicken soup is unlikely to be popular with customers.

▲ **Food needs to be kept and served at the right temperature**

## GIVE IT A GO: hot or cold?

Which food and drinks should be kept hot or cold? Make two lists under the headings **hot** and **cold.**

### • *Table laying* •

Table laying is an important feature of establishments where customers receive their food at the table. Laying up tables is the responsibility of the waiting staff. Each establishment will have its own style of table lay-up and a routine that it requires its staff to follow. In many restaurants the tables are laid up with cloths and cutlery at the end of the service shift, in preparation for the next meal. For example, at the end of the dinner shift, the tables will be laid for breakfast service. The tables are then checked and anything necessary completed at the beginning of the next service shift.

Other smaller equipment is also needed in restaurant areas. This may include trays, for serving and clearing away food and dishes, service utensils and smaller items, such as menus.

## GIVE IT A GO: laying up tables

Look at the illustration of a table that has been laid ready for the start of service. Can you identify all the service items listed below?

- condiments
- cruets
- glassware
- drinks container
- serviettes
- crockery

Can you think of anything that you might add?

Many outlets now use **disposable** tableware. It is simple to use and cost effective, as the establishment does not have to pay for staff to clean it after use – it is simply thrown away. The type of tableware used will depend on the establishment. You would not expect a Big Mac to be served on a solid silver plate, just as you would not expect a dessert that costs £18 to come in a paper bowl with a plastic spoon!

All of these items are seen and constantly used by customers. If a table cloth is creased and dirty and the menu is old, tatty and covered with food stains, it is unlikely to give customers confidence about the quality of food that they can expect. Food service staff are responsible for maintaining these items and making sure they are presented to customers in the best possible condition. It is very important not to use chipped or damaged tableware. Not only does this create a bad image, but sharp edges could cut a customer.

# Delivering customer orders

Although many different people work in a catering establishment, it is usually only the waiting staff that come into contact with customers. They are, therefore, the representatives of the whole establishment.

## Communication skills

The duties of waiting staff are all customer-orientated. How they come across to customers will have a large impact on their overall experience. Good verbal and non-verbal communication skills are essential and must be used by waiting staff throughout the service period. You first looked at these in Unit 3. In this section you will explore how these skills are used in food service.

### • *Meeting and greeting customers* •

The first contact with customers will be when you greet them and welcome them to the establishment.

### ... *you were ignored by the waiting staff in a restaurant?*

Imagine that you walked into a restaurant and the waiting staff ignored you and continued chatting among themselves. How would you feel as a customer?

Body language, or non-verbal communication, is a vital aspect of the communication skills for food service personnel. Positive body language must be practised at all times to help customers feel relaxed and enjoy their experience.

Good customer care will help keep your customers satisfied. Many people have favourite restaurants that they go back to regularly.

▲ The first contact with customers is when you greet and welcome them

### ⬭ THINK ABOUT IT

Why do customers like to be remembered by waiting staff?

## GIVE IT A GO: recapping on body language

What do we mean by positive body language? Working with a colleague, copy and complete the table with types of body language customers would see as positive and negative.

| Positive body language | Negative body language |
|---|---|
| Smiling | Scowling |
|  |  |
|  |  |
|  |  |
|  |  |
|  |  |
|  |  |

### ● *Taking an order* ●

Food service staff also need to use their communication skills when taking customers' orders. While taking an order, a waiter or waitress may need to:

- ▭ *identify customers' needs*
- ▭ *provide information on the menu*
- ▭ *take instructions about how customers would like their orders to be cooked.*

Food service staff will have to deal with a wide range of customers. Every customer will be different and will need to be treated as an individual to ensure that he or she gets the service required.

## GIVE IT A GO: identifying customers' needs

Think back to your to your studies in Unit 3, where you looked at the range of customers. Write a list of the types of customer who may require extra attention from the waiting staff. What might their individual needs be? Remember they may not all be concerned with the food and drink.

A very important role of all service staff is to sell food and drink items to customers. Customers may not always understand what all the dishes on a menu are. If the member of staff can describe dishes in an informative and knowledgeable manner, the customer is far more likely to choose that particular dish. The waiting staff need to explain dishes clearly to customers and make recommendations, if asked. Some of the questions that a member of the food service staff might get asked about a menu are:

- *what the name of a dish means*
- *what a dish is made from*
- *how a dish is cooked*
- *what is in a sauce*
- *if a dish contains, for example, garlic.*

## WHAT **if?**

### ... a customer asked you what Tournedos Rossini is?

Imagine you are at work as a member of the food service staff in a French restaurant. A customer politely asks you what the *Tournedos Rossini* is. You are not sure of the answer. What will you tell them?

Where food orders are written down, they must be legible for all to read. If the order system is an electronic one, as with electronic order pads or a computerised system, care must still be taken to ensure that the correct information is input. If a waiter writes down an order wrongly or forgets to include an item, it could lead to the customer getting the wrong order.

### ● *Other situations* ●

As well as actually taking customers' orders, there are three other distinct areas in which waiting staff use their communication skills when dealing with customers:

- *customer enquiries*
- *incidents and problems*
- *customer complaints.*

▲ **Food orders need to be legible!**

## GIVE IT A GO: dealing with customers

Copy the table below and make a list of the type of things that would fall into each category when dealing and communicating with customers. Examples are provided.

| Customer enquiries | Incidents and problems | Customer complaints |
|---|---|---|
| 'What time is it?' | 'Excuse me, I've spilt my wine all over the table.' | 'Waiter, there's a hair in my food.' |
| | | |

### ● *Communicating with colleagues* ●

During the period of service the waiting staff will be communicating constantly with other team members and with the chefs and staff in the kitchen.

Service staff are responsible for passing on customers' orders correctly to the kitchen staff. They will need to advise the kitchen staff about any specific customer instructions about the dishes that they have ordered. For example, a customer might state that he or she is allergic to a certain food, such as garlic or nuts, and ask the waiter to ensure that the product is not used in any of their dishes. Imagine if the waiter then forgets to tell the chef about this! An extreme allergic reaction could even cause the death of the customer.

▲ Lack of communication could have dire consequences

## EVIDENCE ACTIVITY P3 M1

### *You're the customer*

Working in pairs, role play the meeting, greeting and seating of a customer in a restaurant. One of you is the customer and the other is the waiter or waitress.

You will need a real menu for this role play. You could use one from your college restaurant or any other establishment in your area. Spend some time preparing for your role play by studying the menu and checking that you understand all the terms.

Make sure that you cover the following stages:

• seating the customer

• providing him or her with a menu

• giving him or her time to study the menu

• answering any questions about the menu

• taking the order.

At the end of the role play discuss with your partner how he or she felt about your customer care and communication. When you are finished, reverse the roles and have another go!

## Styles of service

There are many different ways to serve food and beverages. How this is done in any catering establishment will depend upon a number of things:

- *type of establishment – you would not expect the food to be served the same way in a fast-food outlet like McDonald's as it would be in a luxury five-star hotel*
- *type of customer – you might serve a student in a canteen differently to a guest at a wedding*
- *type of food being served – snack foods can be served differently to a full meal*
- *number of staff compared to customers – some methods of service require more staff than others*
- *time available – at lunch time people usually have less time than at dinner*
- *type of premises or building being used – what is practical depends on the space there is and this will be different, for example, for a meal served onboard an aircraft, in a roadside café or a five-star hotel*
- *type of equipment available – if you are going to offer food that is silver served, you will need the right equipment (you will look at this later in the unit).*

Fish and chips is a good example of how food service can vary between different establishments. At Rick Stein's Seafood Restaurant in Padstow, Cornwall, they serve the following:

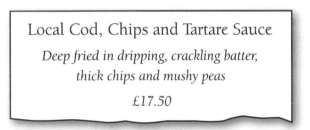

Local Cod, Chips and Tartare Sauce

*Deep fried in dripping, crackling batter, thick chips and mushy peas*

£17.50

You would expect fish and chips to be served slightly differently at your local chippy. You might pay £3.50 and your order would be served over the counter in a newspaper with a plastic chip fork!

It is important for catering establishments to understand the method of food service that is most appropriate for the customers that it is serving.

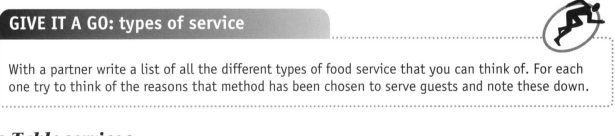

## GIVE IT A GO: types of service

With a partner write a list of all the different types of food service that you can think of. For each one try to think of the reasons that method has been chosen to serve guests and note these down.

### • *Table service* •

This refers to when customers are seated at their table and the food is brought to them by waiting staff. This can be:

▭ ***plated*** – *where the food is assembled on the plate in the kitchen*

▭ ***family service*** – *where the main dish is plated for a customer, but the vegetables are placed in a dish for customers to help themselves*

▭ ***silver service*** – *this is a form of table service where the complete meal is served to customers at their table from **platters**, by waiters using silver service utensils, such as spoons and forks.*

## CASE STUDY – THE RITZ, LONDON

The magnificent Ritz Restaurant is one of the most beautiful dining rooms in the world and is an unforgettable experience for all who dine there. A superb blend of fine **cuisine** and legendary service has made The Ritz one of the most sought after places to dine. Less formal luncheons and receptions can be enjoyed during the warmer months in the private terrace and Italian garden. The Ritz,

London, has a **formal dress code** in its public areas. Gentlemen are requested to wear a jacket and tie when using The Ritz Restaurant. (Jeans and/or training shoes are not permitted in these areas.)

Source: http://www.theritzlondon.com/restaurant/index.asp

In such luxurious surroundings anything less than full silver service would be totally inappropriate. With a main course usually costing over £30, customers will be expecting the very finest service as part of their dining experience.

● List the other reasons why silver service is the most appropriate method of serving the food at The Ritz.

## ● *Counter service* ●

This is where a customer collects their food from a food service counter. There are various types of counter service:

▢ *Carvery*: *Customers choose meat carved from large joints in a heated display area. They then help themselves to a selection of vegetables, accompaniments and other courses.*

▢ *Self-service counter*: *Customers can walk along the service area and choose from a range of hot and cold dishes and beverages. This is the method of service that is typically used in motorway cafés and service-based canteens, such as in offices and colleges.*

▢ *Single point*: *Customers collect everything from one place. This is used in fast-food outlets, such as McDonald's. You are given your Big Mac, fries, drink and dessert all from the same area by one member of the food service team.*

▲ **Self-service is often used in colleges and offices**

---

### CASE STUDY – THREE HORSESHOES CARVERY

The carvery offers a traditional country inn eating atmosphere with traditional country dishes and a selection of fine cooked meats. A whole range of food is available from light snacks to full meals. With some dishes, you can also help yourself to our salad servery, which offers a large range of vegetables and dips. A limited menu is provided on the tables in the bar and extra dishes are listed on the blackboards behind the serving area.

**What to do**

1 Find a table, order a drink from the bar and generally get settled in.

2 Select your choice of food from the menu on your table or one of the blackboard specials.

3 Place and pay for your food at the food order counter, located opposite the carvery. If you wish, you may open an account (credit/debit card required).

4 Make your way to the carvery after your ticket number appears on one of the monitors. Starters and baguettes will be served to your table.

5 At the end of your visit please pay off your account at the food order counter.

● How does this style of establishment differ from that of the Ritz?
● Would this style of service require more or less staff than the silver service method?
● How would the amount of staff being used affect the business and the customers?

▲ Room service is often available in hotels

## • *Other types of service* •

*Room service* is often available in hotels. The room service menu will be placed in all guest rooms. Where the customer does not want to eat in the hotel's restaurant, for whatever reasons, the food can be delivered and served in their hotel bedroom.

*Tray service* is a form of food service where the order is placed on a tray and taken to the customer.

*Trolley service* is where the food and beverages are taken to customers on trolleys from where they can make their choices. For example, restaurants may have a dessert trolley.

### GIVE IT A GO: kinds of food outlets

Why are there so many different kinds of food outlets? Discuss this with your group and your tutor.

### EVIDENCE ACTIVITY  P1

**What do you need to serve food?**

Choose two different types of food service outlet.

Using a suitable IT format, describe the appropriate food service items and equipment that are needed to prepare the service area in these different outlets.

Explain what each item of equipment is used for, and any specific health and safety issues that apply to it.

## Types of food and beverages

The range of food and drink items now available to customers in food establishments and restaurants throughout the UK is huge.

Many restaurants provide full menus that offer:

- *starters – small dishes that a customer may have at the beginning of their meal, e.g. prawn cocktail, pâté, soup or deep-fried cheese wedges*
- *main courses – the food served as the central part of the meal; often the only course ordered*
- *vegetable accompaniments and salads – side orders may be served with a main course or ordered separately*

◻ *puddings and sweets – the dessert course may be cooked or chilled, e.g. apple pie, hot chocolate soufflé, fruit flans and ice creams.*

Some establishments may offer a menu of smaller snack type items, for example a bar menu at a pub or a kiosk in a theme park. Many others specialise in one kind of item. For example, you can find establishments nowadays that offer only soups and accompaniments, such as bread. Others offer just cold foods, such as sandwiches and salads.

## GIVE IT A GO: outlets in your area

Working with colleague, choose an area close to where you are studying and produce a list of all of the food service outlets in that area.

• Note the type of food each offers.

• Note how the customer is served with their food.

Discuss your findings with your group and your tutor.

The range of beverages served in different kinds of food outlet is just as wide. Beverages that may be offered to customers include:

◻ *hot beverages – e.g. tea, coffee and hot chocolate*
◻ *cold drinks – e.g. fizzy drinks (often referred to as carbonated), juice, squash, milk or iced water*
◻ *alcoholic – e.g. wines and spirits. The provision and service of alcoholic beverages is covered by licensing regulations. These state who can be served alcoholic beverages, from where they can be sold, and at what times.*

Did you know that coffee has replaced tea as the nation's favourite drink?

## Service

Waiting staff must have the appropriate skills and knowledge to serve items correctly. For example, white wine that is served warm would not be very well received by the customer who is looking forward to a cool refreshing glass of wine. Waiting staff also need to know what accompaniments and condiments go with the item being served. For example, roast beef is simply not the same without the offer of horseradish sauce!

## GIVE IT A GO: accompaniments

What might you expect to accompany the foods listed below?

| curry | roast lamb | spaghetti bolognese | deep-fried fish |

171

Another important role of the waiting staff is making sure that the food and drinks are at the correct temperature.

## GIVE IT A GO: correct storage temperatures

As you saw in Chapter 7, there are legal requirements for the temperature foods must be kept at.

What temperature must hot food be kept above?

What temperature must cold food be stored below?

**▲ Flambé work is highly skilled**

Watching the skills of a well-trained waiter or waitress serving you is, for many, an enjoyable part of the dining experience in a restaurant. *Flambé* work, for example, is a highly skilled area of food service. Such famous dishes as *Steak Diane* and *Crêpes Suzette* are dishes that were originally designed to be cooked by service staff at a customer's table.

### ● *Timing* ●

All service staff must understand the importance of timing. It is crucial that customers receive the food they order as quickly as possible and in the correct order. Hot food needs to be served hot! No customer is going to be impressed if they are offered a dessert before they have had their main course, or if half a party at a restaurant is served and finish eating before the rest of the group.

### ● *Display* ●

Some food and beverage items may be kept on display in a restaurant. Items such as wine, if carefully and attractively presented, can add to the appeal of the restaurant and help to encourage customers to buy the products. Any such area must, though, be kept in immaculate condition. If not, it may produce a negative effect on customers instead!

### ● *Maintaining the food service area* ●

This is another important aspect of the duties of food service staff. Staff need to work as a team to ensure that the food service area is clean and tidy throughout service and that there are enough supplies of crockery, cutlery and condiments, as well as beverage items, such as wine and soft drinks. If the establishment is one that uses disposables in this area, then a minimum level of stock of such items is still required.

**EVIDENCE ACTIVITY** **P4** **M2** **D1**

### Keeping a log of your skills

As you did in Unit 7, keep a record of the food service work that you undertake as part of your practical sessions. You may want to adapt the evidence sheets to meet your specific needs for this activity (see below).

You can use the sheets to provide evidence of:

- serving a range of food and beverage items using an appropriate style **P4**
- a range of food service skills for different customers **M2**
- excellent and confident practical skills in a **D1** range of different food service situations.

Ensure that you get your tutor or an assessor to sign your forms to agree that you have completed the work to the required standard.

**Practical Evidence Sheet**

| Candidate's name | | | |
| --- | --- | --- | --- |
| Evidence gathered in relation to Unit 8 Food service with a smile | | | |
| Date | Tasks undertaken | Skills demonstrated | Assessor's initials and comments |

# Clearing the food service area

Wherever they are employed, a key role of waiting staff is helping to maintain the order and cleanliness of the areas in which they work. Whether it is a five-star hotel or a fast-food restaurant, any establishment that serves food will have a table clearing system.

Dining and service areas must be left clean in order to:

- *prevent accidents*
- *prevent the growth of bacteria*
- *prevent pests, such as flies*
- *prevent unpleasant odours*
- *maintain customer satisfaction and expectations*
- *provide a clean and organised environment for staff on the next shift*
- *help comply with food safety law.*

## Customer area

The method used to clear tables and food areas must be **unobtrusive**, quiet and quick. Customers do not want to be left with dirty plates on their tables, nor do they want to be overly disturbed by the waiting staff who are clearing away the dishes. There is nothing more off-putting to customers than the sight of tables with other customers' dirty plates that have not been cleared away.

Tables need to be cleared of all waste food, used crockery, cutlery and glassware. This is sent through to the wash-up area, where it can be cleaned and then stored correctly for future use. Any equipment needs to be removed and stored appropriately for future use. This might include pepper mills or high chairs, if an infant has been present at the table. Depending on the establishment procedures, tablecloths may be taken off and laundered, or **slip cloths** may be changed. All equipment and tables must be appropriately cleaned and sanitised, following the guidelines from Unit 7, to ensure maximum food safety.

## Service area

Food service staff need to ensure that the service area is clean and ready for future use. Food and beverage service items must be removed and any items stored if necessary. All rubbish, used disposables and food waste must be disposed of correctly to ensure high standards of hygiene. All bins should be emptied regularly. Rubbish bins should also be disinfected on a regular basis, so that pests are not attracted.

> **GLOSSARY**
>
> **Unobtrusive** means done in a way that does not attract attention.

> **GLOSSARY**
>
> **Slip cloths** are a special covering that is laid over a table cloth to help keep it clean. The slip cloth is smaller than the main table cloth and easier and cheaper to clean.

**WHAT if?**

### ... you were asked to clear away the desserts in a chilled unit?

You are a waiter in a local restaurant. At the end of service the manager asks you to clear and clean the refrigerated unit that is used to display desserts in the restaurant. The establishment procedure is to return all usable food to the kitchen. You notice that a glass bowl full of fruit salad is chipped and cracked. What should you do with it and why?

## THINK ABOUT IT

What must all food handlers do immediately after they have handled rubbish or touched rubbish bins?

Before cleaning, all electrical equipment must be switched off and unplugged. This includes most beverage dispensers, hotplates, plate warmers and any refrigerated units, which must all be cleaned according to the manufacturers' instructions.

## EVIDENCE ACTIVITY  P2 P5

### Induction for new staff

Write a simple set of guidelines to be used by a new member of staff, covering the following key aspects of a service period:

- how to maintain the service area during the period of service, including areas such as the wine or coffee station
- how to clear the food service area appropriately after service.

Think about what is a good order to do the various tasks in.

# Professional, safe and hygienic working practices

This section looks at professional working practices in food service and you will think about how the role relates to ensuring food safety.

## Professional

Serving food and drink to paying customers requires skill and professionalism. In this section you will think about the standards that are required.

### ● *Dress codes and PPE* ●

Waiting staff will usually have to follow a dress code. This might be as follows:

- *black skirt or trousers*
- *white shirt*
- *apron*
- *black waistcoat.*

In a more informal type of service, there might be a uniform especially designed for that particular company. Clothes worn for food service must be clean and should not be worn outside the service area, as they quickly become contaminated with dirt. Service staff must have high standards of personal presentation. This gives customers an immediate and lasting image of the establishment. You are unlikely to go in and order food where you see the waiting staff in dirty uniforms.

As you saw in Unit 7, personal protective equipment (also known as PPE) is an important aspect of working in the hospitality industry. Waiting staff do not need to wear the same level of protection as a chef, but they do face some hazards, such as when handling hot dishes in the kitchen and during service. As with chefs, while on duty they rely on protective items, such as cloths for picking up hot items and strong shoes, often with reinforced toecaps. Waistcoats also provide extra protection, as do long-sleeved shirts.

## GIVE IT A GO: the benefits of a dress code

Can you think of the benefits of waiting staff wearing a special set of clothing? Write a list with a partner and discuss your thoughts with your tutor.

### • *Teamwork* •

In earlier units you have looked at the importance of teamwork in the hospitality, travel and tourism sector. Working effectively with colleagues involves:

- *carrying out written and verbal instructions*
- *keeping team members informed about customer requests*
- *being friendly*
- *helping colleagues if needed*
- *helping to solve problems.*

## GIVE IT A GO: teamwork in food service

Imagine that you are part of a small team of food service staff. How would each of the aspects of teamwork listed above be used by your team during periods of service. How would they be of benefit to you and your team?

# EVIDENCE ACTIVITY

## *Working with others*

During this and your other food service sessions you will be able to generate and record evidence that shows your ability to work effectively with others. After all teamwork is a key feature in all food service operations. This evidence can be used towards your key skills.

## ● *Personal and food hygiene* ●

All staff must follow the basic principles of good personal hygiene when serving food in any establishment. As you saw in Unit 7, the basic principles cover such areas as hand washing, keeping hair away from food, not working with food when you are sick and always wearing clean clothes. Waiting staff must not scratch their heads or rub their hair – and they must not scratch or pick their nose! In addition to this, food service staff must ensure that they do not smoke near food.

### GIVE IT A GO: a food safety quiz

As you saw in Unit 7, by law all food handlers require knowledge of food safety. Working in small groups, revisit Unit 7 and make up ten questions for a quiz on food safety. When you have made up your questions, have a quiz with the whole study group.

## ● *Being attentive* ●

Part of providing professional service as waiting staff is being attentive to the wishes of your customers. You first looked at this in Unit 3. Waiting staff need to make sure that they know:

- ▭ *what the customer wants*
- ▭ *what the customer expects*
- ▭ *how much the customer requires*
- ▭ *where the customer wants to be served*
- ▭ *when the customer wants to receive his or her order*
- ▭ *how the customer is to be billed for the order.*

## ● *Knowledge of the menu* ●

Customers expect food service staff to be well informed about the menu. Waiters need to be able to guide customers through the menu. They may be asked to make recommendations and suggest accompaniments to go with the food. They need to have a good knowledge of the dishes served and terms used in a menu. You looked at professional cooking terminology in Unit 8. If you do not know a term, as in the example of *Tournedos Rossini* earlier in this unit, the obvious thing to do would be to ask another member of the team. The longer you work in the industry, the more you will build up your knowledge of these terms.

### ● *Working cleanly and tidily* ●

As we have discussed in previous units, it is vital that food service staff understand the importance of, and are able to work in a clean, efficient and tidy manner. Anything else will result in a lowering of food safety standards and give a poor image to any potential customers. Poor working practice can also lead to wastage, for example if food and wine are not stored correctly.

### ● *Managing time* ●

Food service staff need to manage their time just as effectively as chefs. Waiting staff are expected to work with many groups of customers at the same time. They need to move quickly and in an orderly manner from one task to the next. Good time management is essential if food is to be taken out to customers as soon as it is ready.

## Safety and hygiene

Food service staff have a vital role to play in terms of safety and hygiene.

### ● *General safety* ●

Waiting staff have a physically demanding job, which involves them moving around the service area carrying hot dishes. They must be aware of safe ways of working in this environment. This includes the safest methods of carrying and serving food and beverage items. They are also responsible for the safe storage of items, such as equipment, crockery, cutlery and glassware.

They also have an important role in making sure customers are safe in the event of an emergency. They need to know the correct fire procedures and emergency exit procedures.

▲ Waiting staff need to work safely

### ● *Food safety*

Many of the working practices that you have looked at already in this unit are essential practices to make sure customers' food is kept safe including:

- *keeping a clean work area and working practices*
- *ensuring safe temperatures for storing food and drinks*
- *maintaining high personal health and hygiene standards.*

As food handlers, waiting staff must follow the procedures you looked at in detail in Unit 7. They are food handlers every bit as much as chefs. All the regulations and guidelines that are relevant to chefs are just as important for the food service team.

**EVIDENCE ACTIVITY** **P6** **M3**

## *Safe, professional and hygienic*

1 Why are these practices essential? Discuss with your group what might happen if you did not follow professional, safe and hygienic food service practices.

2 Produce a list of the possible consequences for you as an individual and your organisation if you do not follow professional, safe and hygienic practices as part of a food service team.

3 Using the evidence sheet from earlier in the unit, keep a detailed record showing how you are working in a professional, safe and hygienic manner, either at college or in your work-place. Ask your tutor or supervisor to witness your working practice.

Check your understanding of the information in this unit by answering the following questions. Then find the answers in the wordsearch.

**1** Personal ........................... is important for members of food service staff. (12)

**2** Looking after customer needs is also referred to as ...........................? (8, 4)

**3** What is another name for a salt or pepper pot? (5)

**4** What is the name given to the disposable or washable cloth that protects the main table cloth? (4, 5)

**5** These are the items served with a main dish. (14)

**6** Wines and spirits are examples of this kind of beverage. (9)

**7** When food is served to customers seated at a table, this is called ........................... (5, 7)

**8** Any staff who work with food served to the public are ........................... (4, 8)

**9** This is the most important thing for any member of the food service team to be aware of. (4, 6)

**10** A basic principle of personal hygiene that all food handlers must follow. (4, 7)

| Q | E | F | O | O | D | H | A | N | D | L | E | R | S | H |
|---|---|---|---|---|---|---|---|---|---|---|---|---|---|---|
| H | P | R | S | O | J | B | W | G | Q | C | N | L | E | S |
| Q | A | M | A | N | H | J | A | S | M | O | U | A | S | T |
| N | S | N | D | C | B | B | Z | R | I | W | L | L | L | N |
| V | J | L | D | L | R | C | S | T | C | P | L | C | I | E |
| G | Y | Z | I | W | C | E | A | K | H | A | E | O | P | M |
| T | E | U | R | C | A | T | M | A | T | I | N | H | C | I |
| M | U | M | W | B | N | S | N | O | G | I | C | O | L | N |
| A | A | P | L | E | X | D | H | H | T | L | G | L | O | A |
| M | T | M | S | D | F | G | T | I | R | S | K | I | T | P |
| O | M | E | C | A | O | E | S | N | N | Q | U | C | H | M |
| N | R | T | F | D | E | B | W | U | A | G | U | C | O | O |
| P | V | E | V | N | Q | C | R | E | C | L | N | W | O | C |
| S | T | N | E | Y | T | E | F | A | S | D | O | O | F | C |
| Y | T | A | B | L | E | S | E | R | V | I | C | E | J | A |

# unit 9

## Planning trips

In this unit you will find out about the information that people will need to know for their holiday or trip and how to give them this information. You will use resources that are available within the travel and tourism sector to investigate different products and services that people buy.

You will use this information to put together plans for trips for all different types of people. You will need to know about the different ways that this information is given to the customer: on the phone, in person or in writing.

Links to websites you may find useful when completing this unit are available through www.heinemann.co.uk/hotlinks (express code 6312P, then go to Unit 9).

*In this unit you will learn about:*

▭ how to use travel and tourism sources of information that are appropriate to planning itineraries
▭ how to investigate the products and services that are provided for different types of customer
▭ how to plan and cost travel and tourism itineraries
▭ how to produce and present itineraries.

# Sources of information

In this section you will look at the sources available and the range of information that different professionals working in travel and tourism need to be familiar with. Information plays an important role in the sector and all travel and tourism workers need to know what sources there are and how to use them effectively.

## Sources

There are many different formats for information in travel and tourism and you will learn about these next.

### ● *Holiday brochures* ●

Tour operators produce brochures to promote the holidays they are selling. There are many different categories of brochures including:

▱ *summer sun brochures, which feature holidays departing in the summer holiday season, from May to October, to mainly European and Mediterranean destinations*

▱ *winter holiday brochures, which feature holidays departing between November and April*

▱ *ski holiday brochures, featuring skiing and snowboarding holidays to both European and worldwide destinations*

▱ *coach holidays, featuring holidays in the UK and Europe, where all travel to the destination, or on a tour visiting various destinations, is provided by coach*

▱ *activity holidays, which include cycling, mountain biking, sailing, wind-surfing and scuba diving.*

The brochures contain attractive pictures of the accommodation, resorts and countries that the customer can choose to visit. Tour operators provide a range of information to help customers decide which country and resort to visit. The brochures also provide detailed information about cost, what is included in the cost, general information on the destinations, the booking procedure and booking conditions.

## GIVE IT A GO: summer sun holidays

Visit your local travel agency and collect three different summer sun brochures featuring holidays to the Mediterranean. Make sure that you collect brochures from three different tour operators, as you will need these for activities you will complete during this unit.

Working in small groups, use three different summer sun brochures to research a presentation for the rest of the class. This should include:

• the different methods of travel available between the UK and the resorts
• the different types of accommodation
• the choices of meal arrangements
• any offers or special deals that the tour operator is promoting
• any additional services provided, such as children's clubs
• what is included in the cost of the holiday.

## GIVE IT A GO: important information

Using a summer sun brochure, list the information that the tour operator provides about:

• destination details
• passport and visa information
• health requirements
• **local customs**
• climate
• currency
• language
• local attractions.

> ### GLOSSARY
>
> **Local customs** are the manners, morals and traditions of people belonging to a particular place, region or country.

## • *Timetables and fare manuals* •

**GLOSSARY**

A **schedule** is the pre-arranged times of operation.

Many different travel and tourism organisations produce timetables for their customers, such as train, coach and bus companies, as well as airlines. The term **schedule** is more common in air travel. The timetable shows the scheduled times that the transport will operate, from specific arrival to destination points. To ensure there is no confusion about the time of day, the 24-hour clock is always used, e.g. 0200 hrs for 2.00 am and 1400 hrs for 2.00 pm Timetable information is available in many formats – printed timetables produced for the public are common for some forms of transport, such as rail travel. The same information is often available on websites or by phone from the service provider, making it accessible to a wide range of customers.

## GIVE IT A GO: train information

Study the timetable which shows the First Great Western service from London Paddington to Banbury. Read the Standard Notes, which accompany it. Then answer the following questions:

1 Which train company operates the service departing from Reading at 1205?

2 At what time does the 1152 train arrive at Oxford?

3 Explain the meaning of the symbol above the train departing London Paddington at 1321.

4 What time does the 1233 departure from London Paddington arrive and then depart from Didcot Parkway?

5 What does the symbol next to London Paddington and Ealing Broadway mean?

6 Are there any connecting services on this route?

### Standard notes

All services are operated by First Great Western Link Turbo Trains unless otherwise shown, as indicated below.

All services shown as operated by First Great Western are operated by High Speed Trains (HSTs) unless otherwise shown, as indicated by **Ⓐ** below.

| | |
|---|---|
| **GW** | Service operated by First Great Western |
| **VT** | Service operated by Virgin Trains |
| **Ⓐ** | Adelante service |

Services highlighted in pink operate on certain days only

| | |
|---|---|
| **MO** | Service operates on Mondays only |
| **MX** | Service does not operate on Mondays |
| **FO** | Service operates on Fridays only |
| **FX** | Service does not operate on Fridays |
| **⊡** | Refreshments are available for all or part of the journey |
| **⊼** | A trolley service of cold snacks, sandwiches and hot and cold drinks is available for all or part of the journey |
| **Bold type** | Means it is a through-service |
| *Italic type* | Means it is a connecting service |
| **a** | Arrival time |
| **d** | Departure time |
| **p** | Previous night |
| **s** | Stops to set down customers only |
| **u** | Stops to pick up customers only |
| **⟵** | Continued from earlier column |
| **⌐** | Continued in later column |
| **🚌** | Bus service. We are not able to take heavy luggage, prams, bicycles or dogs on replacement bus services (except for guide dogs) |
| **⊖** | Interchange with London Underground |

### The 24-hour clock

We use this throughout this guide to avoid confusion between morning (am) and afternoon (pm) times.

For example:

9 am is shown as **0900**

2.15 pm is shown as **1415**

10.25 pm is shown as **2225**

### London Paddington - Reading - Oxford - Banbury — Table 1

| Mondays to Fridays | | GW | ◊ | GW | VT | | ◊ | VT | | GW | ◊ |
|---|---|---|---|---|---|---|---|---|---|---|---|
| London Paddington | d | 1115 | 1121 | 1130 | ---- | 1103 | 1152 | ---- | 1133 | 1215 | 1221 |
| Ealing Broadway | d | ---- | ---- | ---- | ---- | 1111 | ---- | ---- | 1141 | ---- | ---- |
| Slough | d | ---- | 1138 | ---- | ---- | 1134 | 1206 | ---- | 1204 | ---- | 1237 |
| Maidenhead | d | ---- | ---- | ---- | ---- | 1141 | ---- | ---- | 1211 | ---- | ---- |
| Twyford | d | ---- | ---- | ---- | ---- | 1149 | ---- | ---- | 1219 | ---- | ---- |
| Reading | d | 1141 | 1152 | 1156 | 1205 | 1157 | 1222 | 1235 | 1227 | 1241 | 1252 |
| Tilehurst | d | ---- | ---- | ---- | ---- | 1201 | ---- | ---- | 1231 | ---- | ---- |
| Pangbourne | d | ---- | ---- | ---- | ---- | 1206 | ---- | ---- | 1236 | ---- | ---- |
| Goring & Streatley | d | ---- | ---- | ---- | ---- | 1210 | ---- | ---- | 1240 | ---- | ---- |
| Wallingford | a | ---- | ---- | ---- | ---- | ---- | ---- | ---- | 1300 | ---- | ---- |
| Cholsey | d | ---- | ---- | ---- | ---- | 1215 | ---- | ---- | 1245 | ---- | ---- |
| Didcot Parkway | a | 1155 | ---- | 1212 | ---- | 1224 | ---- | ---- | 1251 | 1255 | ---- |
| Didcot Parkway | d | ---- | ---- | ---- | ---- | 1224 | ---- | ---- | 1252 | ---- | ---- |
| Appleford | d | ---- | ---- | ---- | ---- | ---- | ---- | ---- | 1257 | ---- | ---- |
| Culham | d | ---- | ---- | ---- | ---- | ---- | ---- | ---- | 1300 | ---- | ---- |
| Radley | d | ---- | ---- | ---- | ---- | ---- | ---- | ---- | 1304 | ---- | ---- |
| Oxford | a | ---- | 1216 | ---- | 1233 | 1230 | 1245 | 1300 | 1312 | ---- | 1318 |
| Oxford | d | ---- | ---- | ---- | ---- | 1240 | ---- | 1302 | ---- | ---- | ---- |
| Tackley | d | ---- | ---- | ---- | ---- | 1249 | ---- | ---- | ---- | ---- | ---- |
| Heyford | d | ---- | ---- | ---- | ---- | 1254 | ---- | ---- | ---- | ---- | ---- |
| Kings Sutton | d | ---- | ---- | ---- | ---- | 1302 | ---- | ---- | ---- | ---- | ---- |
| Banbury | a | ---- | ---- | ---- | ---- | 1307 | ---- | 1324 | ---- | ---- | ---- |

| Mondays to Fridays | | GW | VT | GW | | | VT | | GW | ◊ | GW |
|---|---|---|---|---|---|---|---|---|---|---|---|
| London Paddington | d | 1230 | ---- | 1236 | 1203 | 1252 | ---- | 1233 | 1315 | 1321 | 1330 |
| Ealing Broadway | d | ---- | ---- | ---- | 1211 | ---- | ---- | 1241 | ---- | ---- | ---- |
| Slough | d | ---- | ---- | ---- | 1234 | 1306 | ---- | 1304 | ---- | 1338 | ---- |
| Maidenhead | d | ---- | ---- | ---- | 1241 | ---- | ---- | 1311 | ---- | ---- | ---- |
| Twyford | d | ---- | ---- | ---- | 1249 | ---- | ---- | 1319 | ---- | ---- | ---- |
| Reading | d | 1256 | 1305 | ---- | 1257 | 1322 | 1335 | 1327 | 1341 | 1352 | 1356 |
| Tilehurst | d | ---- | ---- | ---- | 1301 | ---- | ---- | 1331 | ---- | ---- | ---- |
| Pangbourne | d | ---- | ---- | ---- | 1306 | ---- | ---- | 1336 | ---- | ---- | ---- |
| Goring & Streatley | d | ---- | ---- | ---- | 1310 | ---- | ---- | 1340 | ---- | ---- | ---- |
| Wallingford | a | ---- | ---- | ---- | ---- | ---- | ---- | 1410 | ---- | ---- | ---- |
| Cholsey | d | ---- | ---- | ---- | 1315 | ---- | ---- | 1345 | ---- | ---- | ---- |
| Didcot Parkway | a | 1312 | ---- | 1317 | 1324 | ---- | ---- | 1351 | 1355 | ---- | 1412 |
| Didcot Parkway | d | ---- | ---- | ---- | 1324 | ---- | ---- | 1352 | ---- | ---- | ---- |
| Appleford | d | ---- | ---- | ---- | ---- | ---- | ---- | ---- | ---- | ---- | ---- |
| Culham | d | ---- | ---- | ---- | ---- | ---- | ---- | ---- | ---- | ---- | ---- |
| Radley | d | ---- | ---- | ---- | ---- | ---- | ---- | 1400 | ---- | ---- | ---- |
| Oxford | a | ---- | 1332 | ---- | 1338 | 1347 | 1400 | 1408 | ---- | 1416 | ---- |
| Oxford | d | ---- | 1334 | ---- | ---- | ---- | 1402 | ---- | ---- | ---- | ---- |
| Tackley | d | ---- | ---- | ---- | ---- | ---- | ---- | ---- | ---- | ---- | ---- |
| Heyford | d | ---- | ---- | ---- | ---- | ---- | ---- | ---- | ---- | ---- | ---- |
| Kings Sutton | d | ---- | ---- | ---- | ---- | ---- | ---- | ---- | ---- | ---- | ---- |
| Banbury | a | ---- | 1352 | ---- | ---- | ---- | 1424 | ---- | ---- | ---- | ---- |

Some organisations produce fare manuals. However, these become out of date as soon as fares change. Most organisations now publish fare information on the Internet. This is more efficient as fares can immediately be changed and general information updated as soon as new details are known.

## • *Promotional materials* •

Many organisations in the hospitality, travel and tourism sector produce promotional materials. You have looked at one example of these in the section on holiday brochures. Many different types of organisation in the travel and tourism sector produce leaflets to promote their products and services. Visitor attractions, museums, hotels and restaurants are just a few examples. An effective promotional leaflet will be eye-catching and full of information about the activities and services provided at the attraction. There will be contact phone, e-mail and address details and information on prices and special deals. The leaflet's aim is to entice the customer to visit the attraction or to purchase tickets in advance.

▲ **Promotional leaflets should be eye-catching**

## EVIDENCE ACTIVITY  P1

### Tourist information

Visit your local Tourist Information Centre and collect three leaflets from different travel and tourism organisations. Find the information that each leaflet provides about:

- directions to the organisation
- prices
- opening times
- things to do and see
- contact details.

Make an informative presentation to the rest of your class.

### • *Holiday guides* •

Holiday guides are a valuable source of information. The main professional guides used by travel and tourism organisations are:

▷ *DG&G Agent Gazetteers* – available online at www.gazetteers.com (a link to this site is available through www.heinemann.co.uk/hotlinks (express code 6312P, then go to Unit 9)). Travel agents and customers can get an independent view of holiday resorts and accommodation throughout the world

- *DG&G Holiday Guides* – a series covering a whole range of holiday types and destinations, providing the user with a one-stop source of information
- *DG&G Travel Directory* – the 'who's who' of the travel industry, the website carries full contact details of more than 14,000 companies in the UK and Irish travel industry
- *DG&G Guide to International Travel* – provides detailed information on over 217 countries worldwide, including visa requirements, currency, climate, business and social hints, customs regulations and recommended vaccinations. Available online from July 2005
- *Columbus Cruise & Port Review* – looks at every aspect of the cruise market, from destinations to ship plans and cruise promotion
- *World Travel Guide* – another world destination guide, which contains in-depth information on every country in the world.

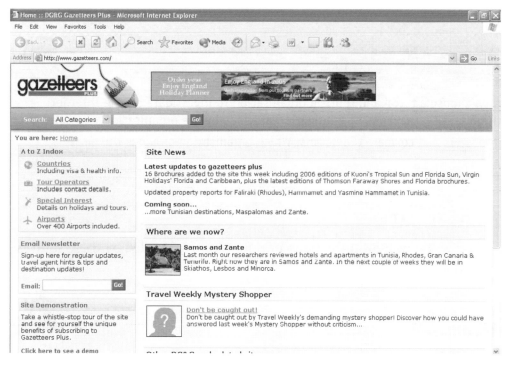

▲ Visit the gazetteers.com site for a demonstration

Organisations that work in the tourism sector may produce their own guides. The following UK national tourist boards each produce a guide for their country:

- *English Tourism Council*
- *Visit Scotland*
- *Visit Wales*
- *Northern Ireland Tourist Board.*

Theses guides provide general information, attractive pictures, prices, accommodation and transport details, to entice travellers to visit their country.

### ● *The Internet* ●

Another important source of information is the Internet. Many organisations and companies have websites which provide detailed information about what they do. Official tourist organisations often have websites that contain links to other useful websites, as well as useful contact phone numbers and email addresses. Most national tourist boards have similar websites to promote tourism in their countries.

Companies that produce travel guides also have websites. Two examples of these are the Rough Guide's and Lonely Planet guide's websites. Visit these sites at www.heinemann.co.uk/hotlinks (express code 6312P, then go to Unit 9).

## GIVE IT A GO: finding information

1 Working individually, choose a travel and tourism organisation to investigate on the Internet. Produce a poster highlighting the range of information provided by the organisation.

2 Display everyone's posters and compare the details. Which organisation provides the most information?

## Information

You will now look at the types of information provided by these sources of material.

## GIVE IT A GO: information please!

Discuss in your group the different kinds of information that a customer might want to know about a holiday.

### ● *Cost* ●

Something that always influences people's decisions when they are buying products or services is cost. This is likely to be a very important factor in most people's decision making about their holidays. Therefore the cost of the product or service must always be available to the customer. People will want to know what they are getting for their money.

## • *Passports and visas* •

All British citizens require a passport to leave the UK. Passports issued to children under 16 years of age are valid for five years and adult passports, issued to individuals 16 years and over, are valid for ten years. Your passport is an important travel document and you need it to prove your identity in the following situations:

- *when entering a country*
- *when exchanging currency*
- *in case of illness, accidents and emergencies.*

Information about passports is available from the UK Passport Agency, and you will look at applying for a passport later in this unit.

### ⬭ THINK ABOUT IT

Why are passports for people aged under 16 only valid for five years?

Some countries require all or certain nationalities to obtain a visa to allow them to enter their country. For most countries, the visa must be obtained before travel. You do this by completing a visa application form and sending it to the country's embassy. A charge may be made and, if so, it must be sent to the embassy with the application. A few countries require visitors to purchase a visa upon entry. For example, to enter Turkey you must have £10 in cash to purchase an entry visa. Your visa is shown in your passport in the form of a stamp or a paper attachment. Information on visas can be obtained from the National Tourist Board or the embassy of the country concerned. Most countries have an office in London and up-to-date information on their website. Many travel agents will process your visa application for you when you make your travel arrangements with them.

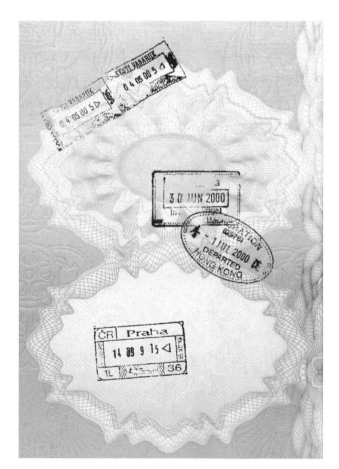

▲ Visa stamps in a passport

## • *Health requirements* •

Travelling around the world always brings some risks to health. Factors which affect people's health when they visit different countries include:

- *the weather*
- *the standards of **sanitation***
- *the different ways food is cooked*
- *the local drinking water.*

In different areas of the world there can be the risk of exposure to diseases that are not present in the UK. Before visiting these countries, all travellers should protect themselves by having the relevant vaccinations. Some countries have strict regulations about vaccination. Some of the major diseases you may need to be vaccinated for, if you are travelling to some parts of the world, are shown in the diagram below.

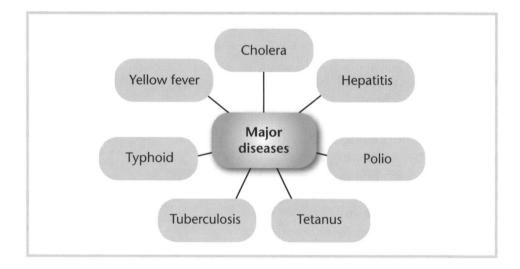

You will find information about vaccinations recommended when visiting countries around the world on the websites of the World Health Organisation and the American organisation, the Centre for Disease Control. Visit these sites at www.heinemann.co.uk/hotlinks (express code 6312P, then go to Unit 9).

The UK government produces a leaflet called *Health Advice for Travellers*. This gives valuable information about how to stay healthy when visiting different countries. Some of the information may be common sense. However, it is important to remember that while you are on holiday you should still keep healthy. The leaflet includes information on the following topics:

- *eat and drink … safely*
- *be safe out of doors*
- *avoid insect and animal bites*

▲ **Health advice for travellers**

- *take care in water*
- *take care on roads*
- *hazardous sports and diving*
- *major diseases.*

*Health advice for travellers* also includes an application form for an E111. This is a document that allows you free or reduced-cost emergency medical treatment in most European countries and some countries further afield. On 1 September 2005 a new publication is being launched in line with the introduction of the European Health Insurance Card (EHIC).

## GIVE IT A GO: protect yourself

Visit your local post office to collect the *Health Advice for Travellers* leaflet. Complete the application form to obtain your own E111 form.

## ● *Other information holiday makers need* ●

Customers will also need to know general information about their chosen destination, such as:

- **climate:** *how hot, cold, wet or dry the country or area is*
- **customs:** *what clothes to wear, country celebrations, days and times of shop opening hours*
- **currency:** *the name of the currency, the different note and coin sizes, the rate of exchange*
- **language:** *the native language and other languages spoken, areas where English may be spoken*
- **local attractions:** *the places of interest at a destination, for example castles, museums and theme parks.*

Tour operators often provide this kind of information in their holiday brochures.

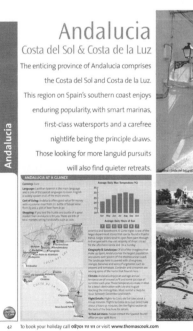

▲ **Tour operators often provide information in holiday brochures**

## EVIDENCE ACTIVITY  P1 M1

### *Worldwide information*

Choose a worldwide destination, that is one outside Europe. Using a range of information sources, independently research and produce an information leaflet to include:

- how often flights operate from the UK
- the approximate cost of flights
- visa requirements
- health requirements
- local customs and languages
- climate
- currency
- popular local attractions.

# Products and services and different types of customer

Every customer is an individual with his or her own needs and wants. We will now investigate the range of products and services provided to meet the needs of travel and tourism customers.

## Products and services

> **GLOSSARY**
>
> A **component** is one part of something.

> **GLOSSARY**
>
> A **scheduled flight** is a flight which operates regularly at advertised, set times, no matter how many tickets have been bought.

Everyone likes time off work to go on holiday. There is a huge choice of destinations, types of holiday and activities to suit the needs and interests of everyone. There are two types of travel:

▷ *package holidays* – *which include two or more of the following* **components***:*
  – *accommodation (hotels, guest houses, tents, etc.)*
  – *transportation (plane, ferry, coach, etc.)*
  – *other travel services (services of a resort representative, transfers, excursions, etc.)*
▷ *independent travel* – *in which the customer books each part of the travel arrangements separately, e.g.* **scheduled flight***, accommodation, car hire.*

## ● *Package holidays* ●

Approximately 85 per cent of the total number of holidays booked by
UK residents are package holidays, which are arranged by tour operators.
The tour operator negotiates prices, timetables and service standards for
the holiday components with other companies. The companies providing the component products – such as coach, flights, accommodation,
car hire – are known as principals. The tour operator then calculates how
much to charge the customer for the components that have been pack-
aged together. An example of what is included in a typical package
holiday would be:

- *flight from London Gatwick to Palma, Majorca*
- *representative to meet customers at overseas airport*
- *coach transfer from airport to resort*
- *14 nights' accommodation at a hotel, including 14 breakfasts and evening
  meals*
- *coach transfer from the hotel back to the airport*
- *flight from Palma back to Gatwick.*

Package holidays are popular as most of the arrangements are made for
the customer. The tour operator is able to negotiate competitive prices
with the principals because of the large number of holidays they are
selling, which means they offer good value for money.

There is a fantastic range of different types of package holidays available
from the UK to destinations around the world. They include:

- *beach holidays – destinations by the sea, where the weather is hot and sunny*
- *activity holidays – e.g. cycling, sailing, golfing, walking/hiking*
- *special interest – e.g. cooking, painting, wine tasting*
- *coach tours – travelling around an area or country and staying at different
  accommodation, with a driver and a guide*
- *fly-drive – return flights to the destination and car hire for the duration of
  the holiday.*

Many tour operators advertise their brochures in the classified section of
newspapers, especially in the Saturday and Sunday editions and particularly if they are a smaller company and specialise in a particular type of
holiday.

# EVICENCE ACTIVITY  P2

## Which holiday is best?

Visit a local travel agency and collect one brochure from each of the five categories on page 193. You could also look on the Internet or send off for specialist brochures. Choose a suitable holiday for each of the customers below and explain why you are recommending them.

1 Robert and Ian like sporting activities and are looking for a two-week activity holiday in the Caribbean in June. They do not mind which island. They would like hotel accommodation, including breakfast and evening meals.

2 Mr and Mrs Brett are in their eighties and still enjoy travelling. They would like to go to Spain and be able to travel around and see different parts of the country with a guide. Neither likes flying, so travel must be overland. They would like a 10–14 night holiday in September.

3 Jackie and Angela want a one-week holiday in Majorca. They would like a beach resort with lots of nightlife. They would like to stay in a three-star hotel.

4 Mr and Mrs Sandhu want to take their two children for their first visit to California for two weeks in July. They do not want to stay in one place all holiday, but to have complete flexibility when they arrive. They have relatives in San Francisco and would like to include a visit to see them if possible.

5 Caroline loves food and wine. She would like to go on a holiday which includes these interests. She would like a one- or two-week holiday in the UK or Europe.

## • Transport •

When discussing transport we are talking about the different methods of travelling between your home and your destination, as well as the transport used at your destination. For many people the journey itself is an enjoyable experience and an important part of the holiday.

▲ Today's coaches are very comfortable

▲ Taxis take you door-to-door

▲ Rail travel is very popular

## GIVE IT A GO: land, sea and air

The different types of transport can be put into three main categories; land-based, sea-based and air-based. One example for each has been entered in the table below, what other examples can you add?

| Land | Sea | Air |
|------|-----|-----|
| Train | Ferry | Aeroplane |
| | | |

There are four main factors that influence choice of transport, these are:

- *how much the traveller can afford to spend*
- *the time available*
- *the distance to be travelled*
- *the purpose of the visit – e.g. holiday, visit friends, travel on business*
- *how easy it is to get to the departure point – e.g. airport, railway station.*

## GIVE IT A GO: the best method of travel

State which method of transportation you would recommend for each client and explain why.

1 Mr Bashir has a business meeting in Edinburgh. It will start at 10 am and end at 4.30 pm. Time is very important, as he has meetings in London on the day before and day after.

2 The Davies family is going to visit relatives in Newcastle for Christmas. (The family lives in Reading). The two children are under eight years old. They are going for four nights and have lots of presents to take, as well as all their clothes and games and toys for the children. They need flexibility to stop when they want on their journey and to get around to visit all their relatives.

3 Mr Owen would like to have a leisurely journey down to Exeter to visit his parents. He does not want to drive as he hates the thought of getting stuck in traffic jams on the motorways.

4 Mr and Mrs Duncan are going to the north of France to stock up on beer and wine for Christmas. They will take their car, but want to travel at a leisurely pace and have reasonable rest periods between driving. They both like to enjoy the scenery while travelling.

5 Mai Kim lives in Aylesbury and is a student at Hull University. She wants to travel as cheaply as possible as she will be making this journey four times a year while she studies.

6 Mark has a fear of flying. He is going to Brussels, Belgium, to meet an Australian friend who is visiting relatives there. Mark wants to get there as soon as possible, as long as it is not by air!

## • *Accommodation* •

Accommodation can either be full service, or self-catering. Full service accommodation includes hotels, guest houses and pubs where meals, housekeeping and additional services like a restaurant, bar or leisure centre are provided. Self-catering accommodation provides facilities for guests to cook their own food and can range in size from a studio (a room like a bed-sit with a kitchenette and bathroom) to an individual private villa (a house with a full kitchen, living and dining rooms, bathrooms and bedrooms, and sometimes a shared or private swimming pool.) Camping, caravanning and youth hostels are also in this category.

## EVIDENCE ACTIVITY P1

### Your local accommodation

What different types of accommodation are available in your local area? Use your local Yellow Pages, leaflets from your Tourist Information Centre, local newspapers and the Internet to compile a directory of accommodation in your area. Include hotels, guest houses, apartments, cottages and caravan parks.

## • *Ancillary services* •

You have looked at the main components of holidays but there are many other services that are provided by the travel and tourism industry to ensure that all aspects of their customers' holidays run smoothly. These are known as ancillary services and cover things such as:

- *passport and visa services*
- *foreign currency*
- *car hire*
- *insurance.*

### Foreign currency

When travelling to another country, you have to pay in the local currency for all goods and services that you decide you want to buy locally. There are a number of different ways of paying for things when you are abroad. In many places you can use your bank's credit cards and debit cards, which is convenient as you then do not need to carry a lot of currency at one time and can withdraw small amounts just as you would at home.

Most travellers like to take an amount of the local currency with them to their destination and to do so they have to exchange some British pounds into that currency before leaving. Travel agents, banks, building societies and the Post Office are among the many organisations that provide this service. The rate at which you exchange your pounds into another currency is called the rate of exchange. This changes daily and each organisation selling currencies decides on their own rates. Many customers shop around to see where they will get the best rate before deciding to buy.

## GIVE IT A GO: international currencies

How well do you know your currencies? Copy the text below and then draw a line to match each country with its own currency.

| | |
|---|---|
| France | Pound |
| USA | Lira |
| Turkey | Rand |
| Thailand | Euro |
| South Africa | Yen |
| Sweden | Krona |
| Cyprus | Dollar |
| Japan | Baht |

▲ **The Euro is the currency in many European countries**

## ● *Passport application* ●

The UK Passport Agency is the organisation responsible for issuing British passports and has seven offices around the UK. To obtain a passport you must complete and send an application form to the office nearest to your home. The standard passport has 32 pages and costs £42. As you saw in the last section, passports are issued for a fixed period only and you must apply for a new one at the end of that period.

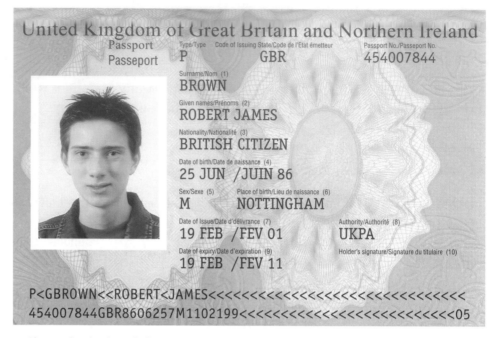

▲ If you don't already have one, why not apply for a passport?

All the personal information on the passport is given on the top half of the page alongside the photograph. This information is repeated at the bottom of the page in a format that can be read by computers. This is used by the immigration services to check the identity of the passport holder prior to allowing them to enter the country. Personal information includes the passport holder's name, sex, date of birth and where they were born.

## GIVE IT A GO: applying for a passport

Collect a passport application form from your local Post Office. Read the instructions carefully and complete the form. If you do not have a valid passport, you could send it off. Ask your tutor to check the form and post it to your nearest passport office with the necessary documents, photos and payment. You will receive your passport in approximately three weeks.

### • *Hiring a car and insurance* •

While many people go on holiday to switch off and relax on the beach or by the swimming pool, other people like to explore. Hiring a car on holiday gives you the freedom to go where you want, when you want to. Hertz, Avis, Europcar and Budget are all well-known car hire companies. The size of the car required usually depends on the number of people travelling and how much luggage they have. Car hire companies give details about how big the cars in each car group are.

The **all-inclusive** cost usually includes:

- *unlimited mileage – there is no limit to the number of miles travelled within the car hire period*
- *collision damage **waiver** – this covers you for damage to your hired vehicle in the event of an accident*
- ***third party insurance** – this provides insurance cover for the injury or damage you may cause to someone or something not in your vehicle*
- *theft waiver – this provides cover for the theft of the rental vehicle, but does not cover personal belongings stolen from your car*
- *bail bonds – this applies to car rental in some countries, such as Spain; if a driving offence is committed that results in imprisonment, this provides money to cover any bail needed for immediate release.*

You may face an airport **surcharge**, if you are collecting your car from an airport.

Travel insurance is always recommended to travellers, as the cover provided includes:

- *medical expenses*
- *cancellation*
- *personal accident*
- *personal possessions*
- *personal money*
- *loss of travel documents.*

### GLOSSARY

**All-inclusive** means that all the component costs are included in one payment.
A **waiver** is an agreement that you will not be held legally responsible for something.
**Third party** is a legal term which means someone other than the two main people, or groups, involved in any situation.

### GLOSSARY

**Surcharges** are an extra charge which may be made for specific additional services.

## WHAT if?

### ... you didn't take out travel insurance?

The Carter family – mum, dad, George (age 16) and Chloe (age 11) – went to Majorca last year for two weeks. They stayed in a three-star hotel in the resort of Alcudia. Mr Carter felt quite pleased with himself as he had saved money by not buying travel insurance, but had ensured that everyone had a valid E111 form, which provides free or reduced medical emergency treatment. Mr Carter hired a car so that they could drive around and see some of the island. Unfortunately, one day the car was broken into and a video camera, a new necklace Mrs Carter had just bought, their passports and return flight tickets, and George's personal stereo were stolen from the boot of the car. The family were unable to make a claim as they did not have full travel insurance. Fortunately, their resort representative helped them to obtain the necessary documents to fly home and arranged for replacement flight tickets.

• Do you think having peace of mind makes it worth taking out full travel insurance cover?

Some banks offer travel insurance cover annually as a free service with the bank account, but most people will need to buy a policy before their holiday. There are many different companies offering travel insurance and their products all differ.

### GIVE IT A GO: travel insurance cover

Collect three leaflets from different companies promoting their insurance policies. You could look for these in local travel agencies and banks.

• Produce a chart to compare the cover provided by each company.

• Compare the cost of cover for a two-week holiday in Europe.

• Which policy would you recommend?

## Different types of customers

You first looked at different types of customer in Unit 3 when you studied customer service. Later in this unit you will be planning travel itineraries for different types of customer. You will think in depth about meeting the needs of different customers, when you plan in detail for their holiday requirements. The following diagram may refresh your memory of the different types of customers.

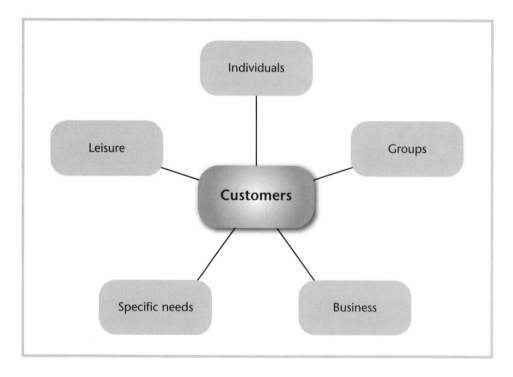

Business travellers are those customers who are travelling on behalf of their company. Employees are sometimes required to travel to meetings, product fairs, conferences, or to visit a colleague in another country. Multinational companies, such as BP, Coca-Cola, Kodak and Disney, spend hundreds of thousands of pounds paying for their employees to travel on business.

Most people are leisure travellers, who travel in their own time for holidays and to visit friends and relatives. Some people travel on their own – individuals. Many tour operators offer discounts or a free place, when there is a group of people travelling together. The size of the reduction depends on the time of year the group is travelling and how many people there are.

▲ **Many people travel with their family**

## GIVE IT A GO: group deals

Compare the group offers promoted in the three summer sun brochures you collected earlier in this unit. Compare three holidays which are similar. Which company offers the best deal?

A customer with a specific need is someone who may require additional help to enjoy their travel experience. The table below details the most common examples of these.

| Specific need | Example |
|---|---|
| Sensory impaired | Blind people may require an escort to take them from the airport check-in to the departure gate as they cannot read the monitors displaying departure information. |
| Dietary needs | Many people are vegetarian. Other diets that a customer may need include wheat-free, dairy-free, Hindu and diabetic. |
| Travelling with equipment | An orchestra travelling to a concert may require additional help with their instruments. A businessman attending a trade fair may have bulky display items, which have to be transported. |
| Travelling with a small child | Additional help could be an airline providing an activity pack for the child and a special children's meal. |
| Physical disability | Someone with a bad leg and using a walking stick may need to sit in an aisle seat on the coach or plane, near to the toilet. |
| Learning disabilities | All the information may need to be clearly written with detailed instructions for both the individual and his or her carer. |

What other examples can you think of in your group? Create a similar table for your file and list two more examples for each category.

# Plan and cost

Many people like to book their travel arrangements in advance so that they have longer to enjoy looking forward to their trip. However, another reason to book early is that you can take advantage of early booking deals for package holidays and flights. In order to get the most from your holiday, you may decide to start your planning early to make sure you can do everything you want to and get the best price.

## Plan

**GLOSSARY**

An **itinerary** is the details of a customer's travel arrangements, such as modes of transport, dates, times and destinations, accommodation, excursions and activities.

An **itinerary** provides detailed information about a customer's travel arrangements. Independent travellers will plan their own itinerary, but may require information from travel and tourism organisations to help them do so. Detailed itineraries will be provided to customers who are taking tours and cruises. Sometimes people may want tailor-made holidays, in which an itinerary is planned to suit their specific travel wishes.

There is a great deal of information that must be included when planning a travel itinerary. Transport and accommodation may be obvious details, but what about meals, trips, visits and activities? Customers also need to know what time they must check in for the start of each journey. Customers must be advised about passport, visa, health, climate and currency information. It is good customer service to include information about local customs:

- *Do the shops and banks close in the afternoon?*
- *Must certain clothing be worn to enter some buildings, such as churches and mosques?*
- *What is an acceptable level of tipping and when should a tip be given?*

## Cost

When putting an itinerary together, you must work out the cost of each component. You must calculate the total cost in order to work out what price your organisation is going to charge for that particular holiday product. You will also want to add an amount for commission (or mark up). This is the fee or profit margin you are going to include in the charge for the work you as the tour operator have done in planning and producing the holiday.

The cost of the following components are added, and then any discounts subtracted to reach the total cost:

- *transport*
- *accommodation*

📁 *food*
📁 *any* **supplements**
📁 *taxes*
📁 *mark up.*

You need to advise the customer:

📁 *what the total cost is*
📁 *the deposit required to make a booking*
📁 *the date the final balance must be paid.*

## GIVE IT A GO: a tour itinerary

Collect a brochure from a local travel agent, which includes tours. Tour operators specialising in touring holidays include Thomas Cook Signature, Travelsphere, Page & Moy and Cosmos.

Select one tour and create a table to show what information is provided about the itinerary of that tour. Use the headings below.

• Tour operator
• Name of tour
• Transport included
• Accommodation
• Meals
• Tours and activities included
• **Optional** tours and excursions
• **Guiding**
• Additional services
• Information on local customs
• Climate
• Currency
• Passport and visa requirements for UK passport holders
• Health and vaccination requirements

### THINK ABOUT IT

Why do you think customers are required to pay a deposit? What is the benefit to the travel agent/tour operator? Can you think of a benefit for the customer?

## EVITENCE ACTIVITY  P1 M1

### *Making payments*

Look again at the tour you chose for the GIVE IT A GO activity 'a tour itinerary', on p.203. Choose a departure date for two adults and answer the following questions.

1  What is the cost for each adult to travel on this date?

2  Is there an early booking discount if customers book by a certain date?

3  How much deposit must each customer pay to make the booking?

4  How long before departure must the final payment be made?

5  By what date must your customers make their final payment?

6  If the customers have only paid the deposit, what is the balance payment for each?

## Specified requirements

There are thousands of different holidays for people to choose from. However, few of us are available to go on holiday at any time. Most people's choice of holiday will depend on their personal circumstances and specific requirements. These include:

- ▱ **budget** – how much a customer wants to pay for their trip
- ▱ **date** – the customer may be limited to school holidays or have specific holiday weeks off work
- ▱ **time available** – the duration might be a one-night stay or several weeks
- ▱ **type of customer** – e.g. leisure or business traveller, family group or individual
- ▱ **number of people** – e.g. two people in a twin or a family group of eight in a villa
- ▱ **purpose of visit** – e.g. to admire the flowers in Madeira in the spring or to take a cruise to celebrate a special birthday or wedding anniversary, or a business person attending an exhibition on behalf of her company
- ▱ **arrival/departure points** – e.g. for someone living in Dunblane, Fife, Glasgow airport may be cheaper to fly from, but Edinburgh airport is more convenient to get to
- ▱ **special requirements** – e.g. a special diet, such as vegetarian, or special facilities, such as a cot in the bedroom
- ▱ **nationality** – may affect the visa requirements to enter some countries
- ▱ **customer preferences** – e.g. a customer might require a hotel in a specific location or with particular facilities, such as a swimming pool

▭ **experiences** – *is this the first time that the customer has travelled abroad or are they a regular traveller?*

▭ **special circumstances** – *e.g. honeymoon trip.*

# Produce and present

## Produce

Once the planning and costing of the components that make up a holiday is complete, you are ready to produce the actual holiday. This involves making arrangements with suppliers for the services to be provided for the actual dates of holidays for customers' bookings.

The supplier is the organisation that provides the product, such as the coach company that provides a coach and driver or the hotel that provides the accommodation and meals. It is the supplier that you will negotiate with to agree what it will provide and how much it will cost you.

When a customer has made a booking, travel tickets are issued for a holiday. They are for a particular **route** and may not specify an exact day or time of travel. An itinerary is produced with details of all the timings of a journey for a customer. For example, here is the travel itinerary for a customer who lives in Southampton, making a return journey to Edinburgh.

| **Wednesday 03 August** | | |
|---|---|---|
| Southampton Bus Station | Depart | 0700 hrs |
| Heathrow Central Bus Station | Arrive | 0910 hrs |
| * Heathrow Terminal 1; latest check-in time for flight | | 0940 hrs |
| Heathrow Terminal 1 | Depart | 1040 hrs |
| Edinburgh Airport | Arrive | 1200 hrs |
| **Sunday 07 August** | | |
| * Edinburgh Airport; latest check-in time for flight | | 1735 hrs |
| Edinburgh Airport | Depart | 1835 hrs |
| Heathrow Terminal 1 | Arrive | 2005 hrs |
| Heathrow Central Bus Station | Depart | 2100 hrs |
| Southampton Bus Station | Arrive | 2310 hrs |

▲ **Example itinerary**

The itinerary shows the departure and arrival times and the latest time that the customer can check in for her flights. The flights would have been booked first and then the coach timetable consulted to decide the best time to leave Southampton. Enough time has to be allowed to make sure that the traveller checks in before the check-in desk closes.

When travelling to other countries you may fly to a different time zone. The time will be ahead if you are travelling eastwards, and behind if you are travelling westwards. You have to adjust your watch to match the local time in your destination. When writing an itinerary, the local time is always used. For example, here is an itinerary for a traveller flying from Newcastle to New York.

**Saturday 22 October**

| | | | | |
|---|---|---|---|---|
| *Newcastle Airport* | *Latest check-in* | 0505 hrs | | |
| Newcastle Airport | Depart | 0605 hrs | | |
| Heathrow Terminal 1 | Arrive | 0710 hrs | BA1321 | |
| *Heathrow Terminal 4* | *Latest check-in* | 0725 hrs | | |
| Heathrow Terminal 4 | Depart | 1025 hrs | | |
| New York JFK Airport | Arrive | 1245 hrs | BA175 | (1745 hrs UK) |

**Saturday 29 October**

| | | | | |
|---|---|---|---|---|
| *New York JFK Airport* | *Latest check-in* | 2000 hrs | | (0100 hrs 30 Oct UK) |
| New York JFK Airport | Depart | 2300 hrs | | (0400 hrs 30 Oct UK) |

**Saturday 30 October**

| | | | |
|---|---|---|---|
| Heathrow Terminal 4 | Arrive | 1000 hrs | BA116 |
| *Heathrow Terminal 1* | *Latest check-in* | 1100 hrs | |
| Heathrow Terminal 1 | Depart | 1200 hrs | |
| Newcastle Airport | Arrive | 1310 hrs | BA1332 |

▲ **Example itinerary**

## Present

Information should be presented in a way that meets the customer's requirements. In most cases the customer will wish to have their itinerary and travel details in writing. This could be in the form of a letter, fax or e-mail. When organising a group trip, information may be presented orally by giving a presentation to all the travellers, then handouts could be issued confirming the details for the people to keep. Some customers do not have the time to visit a travel agent so will make their travel arrangements by telephone, the details are confirmed by telephone and again written confirmation posted to them. An example of this would be a college lecturer booking a student group trip abroad with a specialist company. All the details are exchanged and confirmed by telephone and the details confirmed in writing.

## EVIDENCE ACTIVITY  P2 P3 P4 M1 M2 M3

*Planning travel itineraries*

1 You are now required to plan and cost an itinerary to meet the needs of the following customers. Complete this activity independently using the sources discussed in this unit, and additional travel and tourism sources of information that are relevant. Include all the appropriate components to meet the specified needs of the customers.

   **a** Ina and Antony want to travel from their home near Manchester to Paris for four nights departing Saturday 24 September. They would like to fly, stay in a four-star hotel with breakfast included and have trips and excursions arranged for their stay. They want to see as much of Paris and the surrounding area as they can.

   **b** A businesswoman, Sally McGregor, must travel from her home in Edinburgh to Reading, Berkshire, for a four-day trade exhibition. Her company is arranging for her equipment to be delivered separately, so she would like to fly to Heathrow and then travel by train to Reading. She would like to stay in a four-star hotel.

   **c** Mr and Mrs Hudson and their children – Megan (10 years) and David (7 years) – would like to go to Orlando, Florida, in June for two weeks. They require return flights, three- or four-star hotel accommodation for two weeks and car hire. The car must be able to carry them and four large suitcases. They would like to pre-book attraction tickets to Disneyworld and the other main attractions.

2 Produce the detailed itineraries that meet the needs of the specified range of customers. Use a format that is clear and easy to understand.

## EVIDENCE ACTIVITY D1 D2

*Presenting itineraries*

1 Explain in writing how the itineraries you created meet the specified needs of the customers.

2 Present your planned itineraries in a format that is appropriate to each group of customers and explain orally how they meet the specified needs of each group of customers.

| A | C | G | W | J | M |
|---|---|---|---|---|---|
| B | E | Z | O | K | V |
| S | E | A | R | C | H |
| R | F | I | D | L | O |

Check your understanding of the information in this unit by answering the following questions. Then find the answers in the wordsearch.

**1** The detailed written information giving dates and times of a journey. (9)

**2** This type of holiday could include return flights, accommodation and the services of a resort representative. (7)

**3** The type of organisation that puts the components of a package holiday together and produces holiday brochures. (4, 8)

**4** Aircraft, trains and coaches are different types of ................. (9)

**5** The valid document that UK citizens must have to be able to leave the country. (8)

**6** Vegetarian, dairy and wheat-free are different types of ............ (4)

**7** What do some countries require certain nationalities to obtain to enter their country? (4)

**8** Travel ................. is always recommended to cover travellers for medical and other incidents while on holiday. (9)

**9** Most of the time people are ................. travellers – travelling in their own time for holidays and to visit friends and relatives. (7)

**10** Hotels, guest houses and apartments are different types of ................. (13)

| P | Q | L | Y | O | K | T | A | S | I | V | H | X | D | T |
|---|---|---|---|---|---|---|---|---|---|---|---|---|---|---|
| F | C | E | X | C | S | A | R | X | Y | S | X | I | R | T |
| V | Y | I | E | F | O | C | W | O | D | J | F | O | O | T |
| C | S | S | D | Q | I | C | D | C | P | J | P | U | I | B |
| E | E | U | A | D | J | O | X | V | Z | S | R | H | F | C |
| C | V | R | H | U | X | M | B | V | S | O | N | D | P | J |
| N | F | E | Y | W | X | M | X | A | P | F | I | A | E | S |
| A | G | Y | Y | U | G | O | P | E | R | E | Y | T | R | Q |
| R | S | G | M | W | L | D | R | L | T | J | H | C | V | T |
| U | K | W | N | Y | R | A | R | E | N | I | T | I | G | D |
| S | T | T | Y | A | T | T | P | A | C | K | A | G | E | L |
| N | A | P | Z | O | W | I | W | W | H | D | R | U | P | D |
| I | J | A | R | G | O | O | J | Q | W | F | R | U | I | Q |
| P | C | O | O | C | U | N | C | I | A | R | O | U | G | O |
| O | A | Z | Z | R | D | S | X | U | D | X | D | V | F | L |

# unit 10

· · · · · · · · · · · · · · · · · · · · · · · · · · · · · ·

# Using displays in travel and tourism

There are many different ways that travel and tourism organisations promote what they sell. One way is using displays. In this unit you will find out about different types of display and how they are used. You will need to go to different types of travel and tourism organisations to see the ones they use and find out what is needed to make a good display. You can then use this information to look closely at two displays so you can say how good they are and also use this information to plan your own display. You will be given some information about what you have to promote and then you will have to come up with a plan for what you think your display should look like. Once you have a good plan you will then have to put together your display.

*In this unit you will learn about:*

- ➡ how displays are used in travel and tourism organisations
- ➡ examples of displays used by travel and tourism organisations
- ➡ planning a display for travel and tourism to meet specified requirements
- ➡ producing a travel and tourism display.

# Displays and travel and tourism organisations

In this section you will look at the main kinds of display used in travel and tourism. There is a huge range of display materials available and producing interesting displays is a skilled and creative part of working in travel and tourism.

## Types of display

Travel and tourism organisations use many different types of display to promote their products and services.

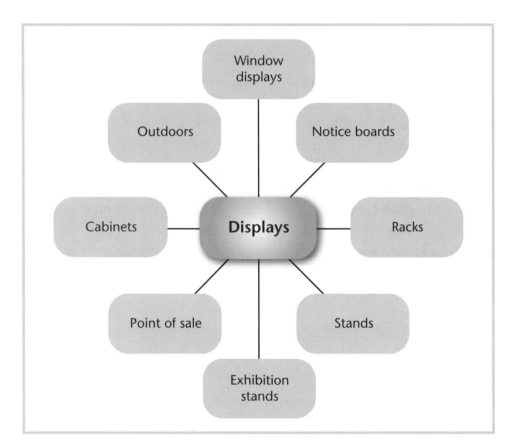

## • *Window displays* •

Windows are very important to travel and tourism organisations. The information displayed in the window should **entice** customers into the premises to make a purchase. Most organisations have a plan of what information should be displayed. This is updated regularly to ensure the window display is always interesting.

▲ **Window displays are very important to travel and tourism organisations**

Travel agencies situated on busy high streets and in shopping centres have lots of different information in their windows. This might include destination posters, listings of flight prices, window cards with holiday deals and discount offers, and a board listing rates for different currencies. The **late availability** cards, for holidays at discounted prices, must be updated at least every two days to ensure the information is valid.

> **GLOSSARY**
>
> **Late availability** means those holidays with departure dates in the next few days.

## GIVE IT A GO: window shopping

In small groups, choose a high street travel agent to visit in your area. Draw a plan of the window display. Include all the different types of information given and describe how the information is presented, for example with coloured cards, plastic screens or **a ripple board**.

Make a presentation to the rest of your class and explain the window display in detail.

### ● *Notice boards* ●

Many travel and tourism organisations use notice boards, including hotels, tourist information centres, visitor attractions and tour operators. These will be placed in a designated area, where they are easily visible for customers. They can be used to promote a variety of information, including late deals and special offers. They provide an easy way to display and update information regularly. Both external and internal notice boards are available. The type chosen will depend on use.

> **GLOSSARY**
>
> A **ripple board** is a board divided into strips which are 3-sided and turn to show different images.

▲ Notice boards display a variety of information

## • *Racks* •

Racks are used by travel and tourism organisations to display large numbers of brochures and leaflets. The rack is normally securely fixed to a wall and ensures the documents are displayed neatly. Racks often have space for headings or titles to be attached to help the customer find the right product. For example, the brochure rack in a travel agency may be divided into areas for summer sun, ski, cruise or UK holiday brochures. The racks in a tourist information centre may be divided to show different types of information, such as local attractions, accommodation, theatre and cinema, or activities. The rack in a hotel may display leaflets promoting things to do and see in the area and also other hotels in the same company around the UK.

▲ Racks are used to display brochures and leaflets

## • *Stands* •

Stands are similar to racks. Rather than being fixed to the wall, they are free-standing and can be placed in the centre of a room to ensure the information on display cannot be missed. Stands often rotate, making it easier for more customers to view all the literature displayed. Travel and tourism organisations that use stands include travel agencies, tourist information centres and transport operators, such as rail and coach companies.

## ● *Exhibition stands* ●

Exhibition stands are large free-standing structures that are often used for temporary displays at an exhibition or trade fair. They are used to promote the products of the organisation to the public and other professionals in the travel and tourism industry. Posters and banners are used on exhibition stands to attract people's attention. Many different promotional materials will be available and might include free promotional items with the company's logo, such as free sweets or stickers. These aim to help the customer remember the company and product.

Some organisations that do not have many high street outlets, such as tour operators and airlines, will use exhibition stands at events like conferences to promote their products, services and special promotions. The stands stay in one place for a limited period and can be dismantled and rebuilt in a different town quite easily. Exhibition stands may also be placed in public areas, such as in an airport terminal or large shopping centre, where an organisation is hoping to attract new customers.

▲ **Exhibition stands are used at exhibitions and trade fairs**

### GIVE IT A GO: travel exhibitions

There are a number of travel exhibitions that take place every year in the UK. If possible arrange to visit one and you will see a huge range of exhibition stands and displays. Below are some of the major UK exhibitions. You can visit these sites at www.heinemann.co.uk/hotlinks (express code 6312P, then go to Unit 10).

- Visit Scotland Expo
- Eye For Travel – Travel Distribution Summit Conference and Exhibition
- Destinations – The Daily Telegraph Holiday and Travel Fair
- International Group Leisure & Travel Show, YPL Exhibitions
- WTM (World Travel Market), Reed Travel Exhibitions Ltd
- Belfast Telegraph Holiday World Experience, Business Exhibitions Ltd
- British Travel Trade Fair, Reed Travel Exhibitions Ltd.

### • *Point of sale* •

Many organisations have printed materials and sample products displayed near to the till to tempt customers to buy the product more easily. A travel agency might have a display of travel books. A tourist information centre might have decorated pens, key rings and note pads that promote the local area all readily available to purchase. When you are visiting an attraction, they might have information about joining their organisation or buying a season ticket displayed at the entry point, with a special offer available if you join instantly.

### GLOSSARY

An **exhibit** is an interesting object that is on display to the public.

### • *Cabinets* •

Cabinets are used to display valuable goods and exhibits. The sides are made of glass to ensure people can easily see the items displayed. Glass cabinets keep **exhibits** clean and safe.

### • *Outdoors* •

Outdoor displays are used when organisations want to make a huge impact so that the customer will remember the message. A good example of an

▲ Glass cabinets keep exhibits clean and safe

▲ Small planes may be seen pulling messages behind them

outdoor display is the kind often seen in holiday beach resorts, when a small plane flies past pulling a message behind it. Perhaps you have seen large mobile displays positioned in country fields beside motorways or large billboards around football pitches. These are also effective outdoor display techniques.

## Travel and tourism organisations

Most travel and tourism organisations use displays to attract the attention of customers. Different types of display suit the business needs of different organisations and you will look at this next.

## • *Travel agents* •

Travel agents use a variety of displays. The most important display available to a travel agency is their window display, which you studied in the last section. This is often what entices customers into the agency to book their travel arrangements. The bigger the window area, the more information a travel agent can display

Inside the agency there will be racks displaying many brochures, which the travel agent will use to help book customers' holiday. Posters on the walls will advertise special deals and promote particular types of holiday and different destinations.

▲ Brochures promote different types of holiday

## • *Tour operators* •

Tour operators do not usually have their own outlets as they sell most of their holidays through travel agents. Tour operators supply travel agents with display materials to use in their agencies, for example brochure racks and huge supplies of brochures.

Customers can also make bookings directly through the tour operator's telephone reservations department or through their website on the Internet. The tour operator's website is an important method of displaying their products and services. They will ensure their web pages look attractive by using bright colours, welcoming and happy pictures and advertising competitive prices.

At the destination resorts, resort representatives will use displays to provide information on services to holiday makers. For example, there may be a notice board to promote local **excursions** and special offers on activities.

### GLOSSARY

An **excursion** is a sightseeing trip.

## • *Transport operators* •

Different kinds of transport operator use different kinds of displays. Bus and coach companies often have displays printed on the side of their vehicles advertising their products and services. For example, they may advertise particular routes and special fares. Bus tour companies often advertise their guiding services on the side of their tour buses. The same information might also be printed on leaflets, which are displayed in racks and stands in their booking offices and tourist information centres.

▲ A popular way to see city sights

Ferry companies and airlines use billboards to advertise their products in places where they will be seen by the public, for example around sports pitches, in town centres and beside busy roads.

### • *Attractions* •

Visitor attractions usually need to use many different kinds of display to provide information to the public. They all produce promotional leaflets to display on their own premises and in tourist information centres, hotels and travel agencies. In popular holiday destinations local attractions will use outdoor displays, such as roadside billboards, mobile displays positioned beside motorways and light aircraft banners, to promote their products to holiday visitors.

They will also produce different leaflets to guide visitors round their attraction. They may use notice boards, which are updated regularly with information about any special activities and attractions. Visitor attractions, such as museums, use cabinets to display exhibits. Many attractions have their own souvenir shops and will also use cabinets to display expensive items safely.

### • *Tourist Information Centres* •

Tourist Information Centres are full of information about local attractions, restaurants, hotels and activities. The details are displayed in window displays and on brochure racks and leaflet stands. Tourist Information Centres often have outdoor notice boards in popular areas of the town, which display town maps and promote facilities and activities in the local area.

### • *Tourist boards* •

Tourist boards exist to promote their area or country. They will have stands at travel and holiday exhibitions, such as the World Travel Market and the British Travel Trade Fair. They will use eye-catching exhibition stands to attract customers' attention. These will include banners and posters showing the highlights of their region and racks and stands to display their brochures. They may also use billboards with attractive advertisements which promote their region.

## GIVE IT A GO: UK Tourist Boards

Visit the websites for the World Travel Market and The British Travel Trade Fair at www.heinemann.co.uk/hotlinks (express code 6312P, then go to Unit 10). Identify the different British local, regional and national tourist boards that exhibit at these exhibitions.

## • *Hotels* •

Hotel reception areas are beautifully presented and often include racks or stands, which display leaflets advertising attractions and restaurants nearby. They may also have displays promoting hotels in other locations that belong to the same hotel group. Larger hotels will have a notice board advertising meetings and functions that are taking place that day and advising which room the events are being held in.

▲ **Hotel receptions display lots of information**

# Displays used

## Purpose and aims

The **purpose** of any display is to provide up-to-date and accurate information to promote a particular product or service. The **aim** of the display is to attract customers' attention and encourage them to make a purchase. The procedure that is often followed to make an effective display is called AIDA. This stands for:

**A**ttention

**I**nterest

**D**esire

**A**ction

> **GLOSSARY**
>
> A **purpose** is the reason for doing something.
> An **aim** is a target you have set, which you direct your energy towards meeting.

## • *Attention* •

Attracting the customer's attention is the most important thing in creating an effective display. Customers must notice the display and be tempted to stop and read the information.

### GIVE IT A GO: take a look

What information is displayed on the notice boards in your area of your school or college? How effective are they in making you stop and read them?

The diagram below shows some effective ways of making your displays stand out.

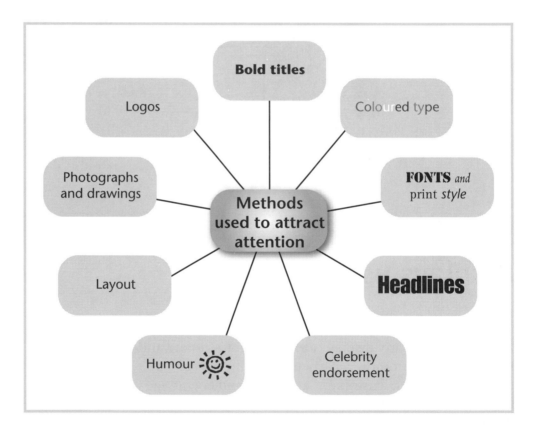

Colours give different impressions and are chosen by organisations to highlight different moods and types of product. For example, summer holiday brochures often use blues and yellows to promote sun, sea and sand. The company easyJet has chosen a bold, bright orange as its brand colour.

What font you choose to use will depend on the information you are displaying. People read displays quickly so any display must be very clear. Some important information, such as departure times or health and safety notices needs to be very easy to read. For other information promoting a local attraction you may want to create an **atmosphere** that suits the particular attraction.

▲ **A good stopping place for visitors, both foreign and domestic**

There are thousands of different fonts to choose from. Just a few examples are shown below:

Arial is often used in text books as it is very easy to read.
But to some people it may look boring!

Chiller would be good to advertise ghost tours or attractions such as the London Dungeon.

Andy could be used to represent a person's handwriting

An unusual and imaginative headline, written in bold type, can really grab the customer's attention.

there's no place like **home**

▲ **Does this advert catch your eye?**

enjoy**England**™

The aim of logos is to catch your attention and make you remember a promotion or display. Some logos include an interesting design or **symbol**. For example, the Visit Britain campaign features a rose.

Good layout is also important as this helps the customer to read your information or find your message quickly and easily. Adverts and posters with 'empty' or 'blank' spaces can be very effective.

'A picture is worth a thousand words.' A well-chosen photograph or drawing to illustrate your text can be very effective at grabbing attention and creating atmosphere.

▲ Sometimes a picture is all you need

If you see a picture of someone you recognise, such as a celebrity like a pop star or TV presenter, you may be intrigued enough to read the accompanying text. Therefore companies often pay celebrities to **endorse** their products to encourage customers to buy them.

Humour is often used to attract people's attention. If you see a picture of something funny, such as a dog lying sunbathing on a sunbed wearing sunglasses, you are quite likely to stop and read the information alongside the picture.

**GIVE IT A GO: attention grabbers!**

Research good examples of the different techniques used to attract customers' attention. Look at a range of brochures, leaflets and newspaper and magazine advertisements. Make a notice board, with different sections to display the different techniques used to attract customers' attention.

## • *Interest* •

Once the customer's attention has been hooked, you have to keep their interest to ensure they read all the information. This can be done by giving more information about the headline. Using humour is a technique which can work here also. Including a special offer or other **incentive** is another good way of keeping the customer's interest.

## • *Desire* •

The third stage of the AIDA process is to make the customer want to buy the product. Having attracted their attention and kept their interest, organisations want to create the desire in their customers. Therefore you need to choose your words carefully when writing. You can create desire by describing the product in a way that makes the customers feel they are already there enjoying the experience. Words like 'exciting', 'tastiest' and 'fastest' can do this because they are words about experiences. Also sensory words – like 'taste', 'smell', 'hear', 'take part in' – make the customer feel they are already there. Sometimes adverts seem like they are talking directly to you because they are using words like 'you', 'your' and 'our'. This makes you feel that it is a special message just for you.

## • *Action* •

The final stage of AIDA is telling the customer how they can take action and buy the product. Point of sale promotions are most effective in this, as the customer can decide to, and actually make, their purchase straight away. The longer the time a customer has to think about it, the greater the possibility that they may change their mind.

## • *Target market* •

You can classify customers into many different types. The term **target** market refers to the group of customers an organisation is trying to attract.

The following companies have markets that are targeted by age:

- *Saga Holidays – for people aged 50 and over*
- *PGL – activity holidays and summer camps for children aged between 7 and 17 years old*
- *Club 18–30 – lively holidays for young people aged between 18–30.*

### THINK ABOUT IT

Age is not the only way of classifying people. Can you think of different target markets that are not connected to age?

## GIVE IT A GO: book now!

Look at the pages from the Airtours brochure, which give the booking information. How easy is it for customers to take action and make a booking?

EASY BOOKING

## CALL
### 0870 241 8981

and connect to our specialist Greece team from the comfort of your own home, at a time that's convenient for you.

**Lines are open**
Mon-Fri 8am-10pm, Sat 8.30am-8pm, Sun 9am-9pm. Please note, when booking by phone, calls may be recorded for training purposes. You can pay direct over the phone using your credit or debit card. No charge is made for using this method of payment. A booking fee per paying customer is applicable, please ask for details. Please note, bookings made by phone are made through Holidayline ABTA 48226, who act as our agents.

## POP IN
### to your travel agent,

for expert face to face advice.

Travel agent helplines.
These numbers are dedicated for travel agent use only.

Travel agent pre-departure helpline.
Holiday Services: 0870 241 2567
Lines are open: Mon-Sat 9am-5.30pm.

Travel agent post departure queries.
Customer Services: 0870 241 2530
Lines are open: Mon-Fri 9am-5pm.

EASY BOOKING

## CLICK ON

you can now browse and book online at a time that suits you. Online discounts are available. To book a holiday from this brochure simply...

1 pick your accommodation from our brochure and note the holiday number detailed in the price panel
2 log on to www.airtours.co.uk
3 scroll down until you find the Holiday Quick Find button... then click!
4 enter your holiday number and chosen departure date and begin your search.

Airtours Holidays, Holiday House, Sandbrook Park, Sandbrook Way, Rochdale, Lancashire OL11 1SA
MyTravel Tour Operations Limited trading as Airtours Holidays ATOL 1179 ABTA V6896

### exclusive online discounts
we'll give you extra money off your holiday when you book online.

### holiday travel guides
everything you need to know about your destination in one place.

### great early booking deals
more choice and great deals when you book early.

▲ **Saga Holidays targets people in their fifties and older**

Lifestyle is another way of grouping people. Examples of this would include the family market and the singles markets, which both have very different interests. Some of the major UK tour operators choose to start their main TV advertising for family summer holidays on Christmas Day. This is because they know that many families spend the festive season together. When they see the advert, they can make an instant decision to book to go away together and have a holiday to look forward to over the winter months.

For any promotion to be successful you have to target your chosen market. When creating a display you need to target in a similar way. A display that includes pictures of someone like you is more likely to attract your attention.

## GIVE IT A GO: target markets

Look back to your examples of different techniques used to attract people's attention, from the activity on p.220. Do these promotional materials target different markets?

## EVIDENCE ACTIVITY P1

### *How displays are used*

In small groups, visit a variety of local travel and tourism organisations. Take photographs of the many different displays you see. Contact the manager and ask for permission before your visit. Make a display board for your classroom to show the different types of display and identify the types of materials each is made of.

# Practical details

## • *Types of material* •

Displays may be made from many different types of material depending on the size, where the display will be positioned, how long the display is to last and what the display is to hold. For example:

⬭ *point of sale leaflet holder – may be made of card or Perspex*
⬭ *window display material – may be large Perspex frames to hold posters, with wire cabling to secure the frames between the ceiling and floor*
⬭ *exhibition stands can be made of a variety of materials, including strong plastic panels, metal poles, felt-covered boards*
⬭ *racks – can be wooden or Perspex*
⬭ *cabinets – may be wood and glass.*

## • *Location* •

The success of a display depends on its location. Displays should always be located in a prominent position where they will easily be seen by as many people as possible. Examples include in the shop window, in the hotel foyer or at the entrance to a visitor attraction.

## • *Duration* •

Different displays will be needed for different periods of time. They can be:

⬭ *permanent – in position over a long period of time*
⬭ *temporary – in position for a fixed period of time only*
⬭ *mobile – can be taken apart and moved to a different site as needed.*

The information on all these types of displays needs be changed and updated on a regular basis.

---

### GIVE IT A GO: types of displays

Consider the types of display you have looked at in this unit and those you have seen yourself. Copy and complete the table below with examples of each type.

| Permanent | Temporary | Mobile |
|---|---|---|
| Notice board | Banner flown behind a plane | Exhibition stand |
| | | |

## • *Information provided* •

Displays provide different types of information and in different quantities. Some may only contain pictures with a short rhyming message, others may be more detailed and give specific information about a product, with instructions to customers detailing what to do to make a purchase.

**EVIDENCE ACTIVITY**

### *Describe, compare and explain*

Identify two different types of display, each in a different travel and tourism organisation.

- Describe each display.
- Compare the two displays. What similarities and differences are there? Which display is better at meeting its aim? Explain why.

# Plan a display

## Plan

It is now your turn to plan, prepare and present your own display. When planning a display you need to think about the following points:

- **Location** – *Where you plan to place your display may help you decide what it will be made of and what size it is going to be.*
- **Type of display** – *Is it going to be a large free-standing structure, fixed to a wall or objects in a cabinet? Is your display going to be inside or outside?*
- **Duration of display** – *How long is your display to last for? This may also influence the types of material you will use.*
- **Types of material to be used** – *What resources do you have? Card, wood, perspex, glass? Will you show photographs or a video? Are there people in other parts of your school or college who may be able to provide materials?*
- **Space required** – *How much wall or floor space do you need for your display?*
- **Health and safety requirements** – *Are there any hazards related to constructing your display. You will have to consider what tools you will need to build your display, such as scissors, glue, hammer and nails. Ensure you read all the user instructions on any equipment. When your display is in place check how secure it is. Can a passer-by walk into it, knock it over or injure themselves?*

> **GLOSSARY**
>
> **Resources** are supplies of materials available to use.

> *Appearance* – *What do you want your display to look like? What do you want customers' first impression to be? Joyful, scared, interested, questioning? What colours do you want to use? How much writing/pictures/space will make the best impact?*

> *Information to be included* – *Make a list of what you want to tell your customers. For example, if your display is advertising an event, you may need: dates and times; price and what is included in the cost; where customers can get tickets and information; when tickets will be available. Are you going to include a leaflet dispenser in your display so that people can take a leaflet with detailed information?*

> *Additional resources* – *Discuss with your group and gather together the materials you will use to complete your display, such as glue, marker pens, pins, staples, coloured card and paper, wood or felt. You may need access to sockets to use electrical equipment. If your display incorporates a video you may need a video camera or, similarly, a digital camera to take photographs.*

## CASE STUDY – THE PROJECT

A group of eight students at Newtown College, who are studying the BTEC Introduction to Hospitality, Travel and Tourism, have just completed the display for their assignment. They agreed what they were going to promote and decided to make a large exhibition stand, which would be placed in the reception area of their college. They carefully planned what each person was going to do and agreed that they would hold a twenty-minute meeting at the start of their weekly lesson to discuss progress and make any changes to their plan.

At least one student was absent at every meeting and another kept promising to complete tasks, but then seemed to give valid reasons why they could not be completed.

Two students worked extra hard outside of the lesson times to ensure everything was completed. When the display was put up, it was discovered that the stand was not steady. The student responsible for health and safety suggested fixing the huge display to the wall. Fortunately the college did allow this.

The display looked great and the students received many compliments on their work. Unfortunately the display had to be dismantled a week later as building and maintenance work had been booked to commence in the reception area.

The students' work was a success. However, some things could have gone more smoothly with their project.

- What improvements or changes would you recommend to them, should they have to complete a similar project again?

## Specified requirements

When planning a display there will be specific requirements that have to be met, such as those listed below.

- *The purpose of the display and aim of the display.*
- *The type of organisation and the type of display required – Is it an indoor notice board or an outdoor banner. Is it to be free-standing or fixed to a wall?*
- *Your target market – What type of customers are you trying to attract? Your display may be to promote your course and your college to prospective students. Are you advertising a school/college open day? You may be promoting an event, such as a music performance given by music students, a show by drama students or demonstrations by the hair and beauty students.*
- *The AIDA process – How are you going to attract your customers' attention?*
- *The specific information that has to be included – What information must be given in the display? Would an eye-catching picture or cartoon give the required information? How much writing do you need to include?*

# Produce

To produce a successful display, everyone in your group must agree to follow the plan you have written. Everyone working together and communicating with each other will ensure that all the tasks are completed by the set dates and that everything is ready on time. Always be careful when using sharp or electrical equipment and follow health and safety guidelines at all times.

**EVIDENCE ACTIVITY**  P3 P4 M2 M3 D2

### Plan your display

Now it is your turn to work in a group to plan and produce your own display. You must write a plan of how you are going to produce your display.

1  Decide what you are going to promote.

2  Identify any specified requirements for this display, including the type of organisation and the target market.

3  Brainstorm ideas for the features of the display. Agree in your group what you are going to do.

4  Discuss design ideas. How creative can you be? What would be really different?

5 Make a list of all the tasks to be completed and share them equally between each person in the group.

6 Write a plan listing the tasks, including who is going to complete each task and by what date each task will be completed. Include in your plan all your health and safety checks. You could allocate the role of 'Health and Safety Officer' to someone, whose job it will be to ensure that all equipment is used and stored safely, and who checks the safety of your display.

7 Now you are ready to move on to producing your display. Make sure that you do the following:

- follow your plan
- meet on a regular basis to check everyone's progress:
  - Are you meeting the dates that you have set for each task to be completed?
  - This is also an opportunity to give each other feedback on how you can continue to improve your display.
- maintain health and safety checks at all times
- leave rooms clean and tidy after each lesson and put all rubbish in the bin
- return all the resources you have used to their correct place, e.g. pens, paper, scissors
- agree on a safe place to store your display between lessons to ensure that it is not damaged.

8 Your team should make a short presentation to the rest of the class or your department manager, to present your display and to explain how you designed and created it.

Check your understanding of the information in this unit by answering the following questions. Then find the answers in the wordsearch.

1 Travel agents try to catch their customers' attention by having an effective ...... ........ to entice them into their agency. (6, 7)

2 The name given to the structure that can display many brochures or leaflets. (4)

3 These are used by organisations that attend trade shows and promote their products in shopping centres and airport terminals. (10, 5)

4 The aim of any display is to attract the customers' ......... (9)

5 What kind of people are used in displays to endorse products and services? (11)

6 The procedure that is often followed to make an effective display is called .... (4)

```
A C G W J M
B E Z O K V
S E A R C H
R F I D L O
```

**7** Organisations sometimes use an unusual and imaginative ........ written in bold type to really grab the customer's attention. (8)

**8** Colour can make a powerful impact and blues and yellows are often used to promote ...... holidays. (6)

**9** Where you place your display is called the ........ (8)

**10** Using tools safely and ensuring that your display is secure are both ...... ... ...... requirements. (6, 3, 6)

```
N W B D A S M T H E T D H W D
O J G I M M U X E P V D E N V
I V D U I B X M L G B Q A E J
T A F S G N W G M Q X T L J Y
N A Q S E O W E K E S S T W B
E R T M F I N D D N R I H E T
T M U K I I T B O K B N A K S
T H Y A L P S I D W O D N I W
A N R D P W T X R S Y G D Q V
W X A R D I F Q M B W P S V A
F E C F B I V D R N E V A S I
H C K I Q P W V A V K L F W I
B K H A L O C A T I O N E T K
X X D P J R C F P A A U T C Y
E X A X K L Z T W J P C Y P C
```

# Wordsearch answers

## Unit 1

**1** Customer service agent **2** Food Safety Act **3** Front office **4** Service industries **5** Sales **6** Franchise **7** Split shifts **8** Tour guide **8** Chef **9** Multinational **10** Brand

## Unit 2

**1** Employer **2** Commis **3** Salaried **4** Flexitime **5** HASAWA **6** Free uniforms **7** Code of conduct **8** Development **9** Appraisal **10** Redundancy

## Unit 3

**1** Internal **2** Expectations **3** Impression **4** Communication **5** Uniform **6** Teamwork **7** Positive **8** Body language **9** Smile **10** Accurate

## Unit 4

**1** Strength **2** Professional **3** Ambassador **4** Curriculum vitae **5** Application **6** Sincerely **7** Job description **8** Interview **9** Black **10** Portfolio

## Unit 5

**1** Environment **2** Conserve **3** Thermostat **4** Wetherspoons **5** Biodegradable **6** Cycling **7** HSE **8** Discrimination **9** HASAWA **10** National minimum wage

## Unit 6

**1** Employee **2** National insurance **3** Credit card **4** Budget **5** Bank **6** Save **7** Salary **8** Payslip **9** Statement **10** Mandatory

## Unit 7

**1** Saucepan **2** PPE **3** Salmon **4** Dry goods **5** Do not misuse **6** Cross-contamination **7** Stewing **8** Mise en place **9** Béchamel **10** Kill bacteria

## Unit 8

**1** Presentation **2** Customer care **3** Cruet **4** Slip cloth **5** Accompaniments **6** Alcoholic **7** Table service **8** Food handlers **9** Food safety **10** Hand washing

## Unit 9

**1** Itinerary **2** Package **3** Tour Operator **4** Transport **5** Passport **6** Diet
**7** Visa **8** Insurance **9** Leisure **10** Accommodation

## Unit 10

**1** Window display **2** Rack **3** Exhibition stand **4** Attention **5** Celebrities
**6** AIDA **7** Headline **8** Summer **9** Location **10** Health and safety

# Index

Page numbers in **bold** refer to key terms.
Page numbers in *italics* refer to illustrations and diagrams.